The G Stands for GUTS

A GLIDER PILOT REMEMBERS WWII

D1603455

Mark B. Bagley

with Marianne Stephens

Hellgate Press
Ashland, Oregon

The G Stands for Guts

Hellgate Press
An Imprint of L&R Publishing, LLC
P.O. Box 3531
Ashland, Oregon 97520

info@hellgatepress.com

Book designed & edited by Harley Patrick
Cover design by Chris Mole
Cover Photo "Wings" by Nicole M. Parker

Library of Congress Cataloging-in-Publication Data

    Bagley, Mark B.
  The G stands for guts : a glider pilot remembers WWII / Mark B. Bagley with Marianne Stephens. -- 1st ed.
    p. cm.
  Includes bibliographical references and index.
  ISBN 978-1-55571-657-8 (alk. paper)
  1. World War, 1939-1945--Aerial operations, American. 2. Bagley, Mark B. 3. World War, 1939-1945--Personal narratives, American. 4. Gliders (Aeronautics)--History--20th century. 5. Air pilots, Military--United States--Biography. 6. United States. Army Air Forces. Troop Carrier Squadron, 49th--Biography. 7. Airplanes, Military--United States--Flight testing--History--20th century. I. Stephens, Marianne, 1966- II. Title.
  D790.B2155 2008
  940.54'4973092--dc22
  [B]

                    2008043203

Printed and bound in the United States of America
First Edition 10 9 8 7 6 5 4 3 2 1

Dedication

To my wife, Mary,
my daughter, Susan,
my sister, Agnes —
and
To all the glider pilots
who gave their lives in
the service of their country

CONTENTS

Portrait of Mark Bagley, taken just before going overseas in 1942

PROLOGUE

I n May of 1942, after having been turned down by the U.S. Navy, I decided to enlist in the U.S. Army. As an instructor for the calibration and maintenance of steamship instrumentation, I had a permanent draft exemption. My request to change this was met with resistance by my draft board. But they reluctantly authorized me, and I reported to a recruiting center near Boston, Mass. To my dismay, they told me to come back at another time; they were busy. I advised them that this was the only damn day of my entire life that I would ever enlist and asked them for an affidavit signed by an officer that said they would not let me enlist in the U.S. Army that day.

They thought about it for a little while, and then asked, "Don't you have any friends or relatives you want to say goodbye to?"

"Hell, no!" I replied. I had said all my goodbyes the day before. "If I can't get in today, I'll never serve, even if it means going to jail!"

They handed me a paper to sign, and after I signed it, they informed me that I was now in the Army. I went through the standard physical exam, and was issued a PFC (Private First Class) uniform. They advised me that my pay would be $21.00 a month. I was then asked to report to the auditorium and select which branch I wanted to join.

When I entered the auditorium, I observed several booths, each representing a different branch—Air Force, Cavalry, Marines, etc. Then I saw a large banner, which in bold lettering had this message: "Join the Paratroops and Earn 50 % More Pay." There was a major sitting at the table in full dress uniform, and as I approached, he displayed a gesture of friendship and invited me to sit down. I stated that I would like to become a paratrooper. He responded, "Well, sonny, have you ever been in an aeroplane?" I took my pilot's license from my shirt pocket and laid it on the table. He looked it over and said, "You are classified as a pilot, Class 1A, and are assigned to the U.S. Army Air Forces. You will leave on the 2:30 train for Biloxi, Mississippi for your Air Forces boot camp training.

The young pilot, circa 1940

Chapter 1

BEFORE THE WAR

Foxboro, Massachusetts

As a young man growing up in Foxboro, Massachusetts, I always dreamed of owning my own airplane. Being the eldest of eight children, I did chores for my mother, and as a teenager I worked at whatever job or jobs I could to bring in extra money for my family and myself.

I got to know a man by the name of Tony Cirello, who owned a flight school at the Mansfield Airport. I did odd jobs for him in exchange for flying lessons.

One day, very early in the morning, I was helping Tony prime the engine of his Liberty Challenger biplane. My job was to stand in front of the airplane and carefully rotate the propeller several revolutions, letting it come to rest on a compression stroke. With this accomplished, I stepped back from the blades and yelled, "Contact!" The engine started immediately and the prop rotated at 1,200 RPM.

The plane sat on a grassy mound, and just as the engine came to life, I slipped on the wet grass and began falling forward towards the propeller. I couldn't believe it was happening, and I saw my life flash before my eyes. I thought, surely this is it—I'm going to die now!

A voice inside my head told me to raise my right arm and press the palm of my hand against the propeller spinner. I had but a split second to react, and just as my hand made contact with the spinner, I pushed myself backwards onto the wet grass. I learned a valuable lesson that day, along with many others yet to come.

I worked for Tony for a couple of years until I accrued enough flight time to solo and get my private pilot's license. My parents allowed me to use the garage on their property, which I made into an

Preparing for takeoff, Plainville, Massachusetts

automotive repair shop. This enterprise gave me enough income to be able to afford my first airplane at the age of 15 ½.

My future boss at the Foxboro Company, Mr. Herschel, came into my shop one day for a problem he was having with his new car. He had been to several mechanics and dealerships, but no one could diagnose it. As a last resort, he came to me. I asked him to leave the car with me overnight and come back the next day. I discovered that the car had a cracked distributor cap, causing moisture to seep in around the points, making it difficult to start in the morning dampness.

Mr. Herschel was so thrilled when I fixed his car that he asked me if I would be interested in working for him at the Foxboro Company. He gave me a job as a clerk while I attended training classes in naval instrument calibration. After two years of training, I was ready to teach the class myself, and that's exactly what I did the following year.

Because I was training Navy personnel how to calibrate shipboard instrumentation, I had a draft-exempt status. My co-workers knew I was a pilot, because they had seen me flying around Foxboro for years. Nine or ten of them had sons killed during flight training. Some were angry that I wasn't flying P-51s in combat on the front lines.

And I too wanted to join the service as a pilot. I had gone to my local draft board and told them I wanted my permanently exempt status changed. But they would not listen. They knew of my position at the Foxboro Company, and seemed to think I would be more valuable in that role.

I then went back to the draft board with a letter of resignation from the Foxboro Company and asked them to make it possible for me to join up. I finally managed to get my classification changed to non-exempt. I immediately applied to the Squadron Naval Airbase to become a Navy pilot. I met with the Boston Naval Selection Board and they issued orders for me to report to Pensacola, Florida, as a Lt. Junior Grade Flight Instructor. I was told to go pick up my uniform, and after doing so, I prepared to go to Pensacola for Flight Officer training.

Because I would be going away and didn't know how long I would be gone, I decided to give my Taylorcraft to my brother Frank. This was easier said than done, because it was wartime and I needed to get special permission to fly the plane from the small airfield I owned and managed in Woonsocket, Rhode Island to the airfield in Plainville, Massachusetts. I called the Civil Air Patrol (CAP) and asked for permission to pass through a "no-fly zone." Without it, I might be shot down.

Their reply was an emphatic, "No!" I was told the plane needed to stay where it was.

I asked if I could take it apart, so no one could fly it. "No," they said, "it has to remain flyable." When I asked if I could put it on a flatbed truck and move it that way, their answer was still no. "You can't fly it, and you can't move it," they told me. The only option they said I had was to hire someone to guard my plane, at $200 per day.

I called my sister, Agnes, and told her the CAP would not let me move the plane, but I was going to do it anyway. I asked if she would like to go with me. Despite the risk of being shot down, she agreed to go along.

I decided to wait for a foggy day, with a ceiling of about 600 feet. Waiting would also give me the time I needed to come up with some sort of a plan to deceive the CAP, should they attempt to follow us or shoot us down. I devised the following plan: if spotted, we would lead them on a wild goose chase. They would see us heading in the direction of Plainville, but we would disappear into the clouds, change direction and head back toward Woonsocket. If detected by the CAP when flying east-northeast to Plainville, we would fly inside

Mark with his younger sister, Agnes, in 1941

the clouds. But, if heading west-southwest toward Woonsocket, we would fly above the clouds.

Finally, the day came. The fog was thick, so I went to pick up Agnes, and we took off. We were flying in the dense clouds when I decided to get above them and look around. Before emerging, I made a 180° turn, so we were actually flying toward Woonsocket. Then I spotted two P-40s flying over Providence, and I assumed they saw us, too.

I dove back down into the clouds and maintained the heading for about twenty minutes. Then curiosity got the better of me and I decided to take another peek. I once again changed my heading 180⁰, and when I popped out of the clouds I could see the P-40s over the Boston area. Once again, I went down into the clouds and turned a 180 for the final time. My familiarity with the route told me when we were just about over Plainville. I descended, put the engine in idle and glided quietly into the Plainville airport.

I had previously told one of the owners of the airfield about my plans and he had the hangar doors open. I taxied right up to the hangar where some of my buddies and I quickly rolled the plane in and shut the doors.

It wasn't too long before those P-40s were zooming over the field. We all waved and smiled. It was a disappearing act of which a certain Mr. David Copperfield would be proud!

There were other lessons learned before the war that would prove invaluable to me as a glider pilot. I once took off from a small field in Easton, Massachusetts, in my 40-horse power Taylorcraft. The ceiling was at 1,000 feet. The only instrumentation I had were the tachometer, altimeter, compass and airspeed indicator. I headed east toward Brockton and the coast, flying at 800 feet. The ceiling quickly dropped to 400 feet and the visibility was down to zero. I climbed to 1,000 feet, still in the clouds, and leveled off. Fortunately, for me, I had a full tank of gas, good for about three hours of flying. With such poor visibility, I did not dare drop too low. There were hills, smokestacks and high-tension wires in the area. I continued flying east, bypassing Brockton, heading for Plymouth about twenty minutes beyond.

Plymouth was also socked in, so I decided to continue flying east and out over the bay. I wanted to see if I could break out of the clouds if I descended low enough, and sure enough, there were clear skies. But it was as if my altimeter was lying to me; it showed at least 800 feet of clear skies. Something inside told me not to descend any lower. I soon discovered that what I was looking at was actually a mirror image of the clouds reflected in the water! It was an optical illusion; the sea was only 400 feet below.

There seemed to be just as many clouds below me as above me and I was looking for some kind of separation between the sky and the water. After about five minutes of flying, I discovered where the mirror image began—that was the interface between the ocean and the sky. That day, the ceiling had lifted a bit and if it held at 600 feet, I could follow the highways and railroad tracks all the way back to Plainville. That is exactly what I did, landing safely, armed with new knowledge of an optical illusion in flight that could save my life one day.

The author with a Taylorcraft at the airport he managed in Woonsocket, Rhode Island, circa 1941

Chapter 2

BOOT CAMP IN BILOXI

Biloxi, Mississippi

My primary attempt at joining the service had been thwarted. After being told by my local draft board that I had been accepted to train as a Navy Flight Instructor, the Naval Board in Washington, D.C. informed me that my application had not been approved because I did not have a college degree. Obviously, they were more interested in a lousy piece of paper than all my years of flying experience. Disgusted with the "system" at this point, I decided I had to get into the service any way I could. Determined, I went down to the local recruiting office at Westover Field to join the United States Army.

I soon found myself on a troop train full of draftees headed for Biloxi, Mississippi. We reported to the quartermaster and were assigned new bedding—sheets, pillows, pillowcases and two blankets. We were billeted in Tent City, eight men to a tent.

The next day, right after breakfast, we assembled and were presented with two-man handsaws and axes. We were told that the CO had issued orders to clear two acres of dense timberland located in an adjacent swamp area. The trees were large, approximately thirty-five to fifty feet tall, with trunk diameters of twelve to eighteen inches. Several larger trees were eighty feet tall. There were approximately fifty men assigned to this work detail. The corporal yelled, "OK men, start sawing! When your tree is in free fall, yell, 'TIMBERR-RR-R'!"

My dad had 100 acres of timberland in Massachusetts, and my brothers and I cut lots of timber. We had plenty of experience in the precision control of placing a tree's fall. I could see the first danger we faced here was the uncontrollability of falling trees; they were dropping all around. The second danger was from cottonmouths—the swamp snakes were everywhere.

I noticed one large tree that was almost ready to fall, and one minor detail everyone had overlooked. When it did fall, it was going to take with it the main high-voltage electric lines, which supplied power for the camp sub-station. I made sure there were no men under the transmission lines and waited for the fireworks to begin. The men making their final cut had no concept of which way the tree was going to fall. All of a sudden, it broke free from its stump with a loud bang and began free falling towards the high-tension lines! The men who made the final cut were in shock when they realized it was headed right for the power lines. Although their mouths were wide open, no warning of "TIMBER-RR-R" came out. The tree landed between the two buildings, cutting the main high-tension wires. As the cables separated, they generated huge blue and red balls of fire four feet in diameter. A tremendous crackle sounded as the live wires jumped around like whips. Each time a wire touched the ground, the blue and red balls would start a fire. It seemed like it went on for hours, but I'm sure it was only seconds before power was shut down. However, a dozen fires had to be put out. Luckily, the camp fire department made short work of that after they arrived on site.

Because of the brilliant CO's decision to use untrained men in place of professionals, the camp was now without electricity. Personally, I was just glad no one was injured—and that no more swamp work would be required!

The next day, I was assigned to KP duty and washed pans for half the day. The balance of the day I spent peeling potatoes. I decided I would never do that again. But how could I avoid it? I came up with a plan. I would put myself on KP. Instead of going to the kitchen, I went to the food warehouse and looked around. I saw boxes of all kinds of fruit and sacks of flour and sugar. I got a hand truck and relocated half of the apples to the other end of the warehouse. Then I sat down to enjoy whatever I fancied. Milk, apples, bananas . . . nothing was off limits.

The door opened and a sergeant came in, wanting to know what I was doing. I replied that some corporal wanted these apples stored in one place and that I was "consolidating the inventory" by moving them to one area. "OK, soldier. Carry on," he said as he departed.

*   *   *

Boot camp training included about a week of close order drills. The drill instructor was an obnoxious little corporal, with one hell of a loud voice. He managed to get us so mad that we wanted to "take it outside," just to give him some of his own insults.

After about a week of close order drill instruction, we were able to pass muster and went on to target practice, using old 30-30, 1906 Springfield rifles. Next came our introduction to gas warfare. They gave us gas masks, and there were special tents that we were expected to use in the event of a gas attack. There were various gas chambers, each with a specific type of gas, i.e. mustard gas, Phosgene, etc. These were not real, but simulated, and we were to identify each gas by its smell (e.g., mustard gas smells like rotten eggs). After identifying the gas, we could leave the chamber. The gas tent was to be used during a rainstorm gas attack, to prevent clothing from becoming saturated with chemicals and reaching the skin.

The next series of trainings were all about sexual conduct. Without going into detail, we watched films about various venereal diseases. We would not be issued any passes unless we had condoms in our possession. Anyone then using a condom had to report to the medics for additional prophylactic treatment.

At our last class, the instructor asked, "Who wants a pass?" There was no response. None of us wanted to be the first to ask for a supply of condoms. I for one had never seen or used one, and many of the men must have been in the same position. No one would ask for any, but I really wanted to go into town. So I asked for a prophylactic kit. The instructor asked me how many kits I wanted. I replied, "About six will do for today . . ." Then everyone started asking for their kits.

The first trip into town was a doozie! An acquaintance in my tent was a good swimmer and invited me to go swimming in Biloxi. I told him I could not swim, but he said, "It's simple! Just jump in and swim!" We put our swimsuits on under our uniforms and went into town. There was a long pier extending into the gulf, and my buddy decided it was a good location for a beginner. At about fifty to sixty feet from shore, I decided to go no farther. That was my limit. My friend assured me that he would be at my side if I required help. I took a deep breath and jumped in. I went under for the first time and came up; my buddy was nowhere in sight! As I went down for the second time, I remembered what my mother told me on one of our visits to a nearby lake. When I was ten years old, she had tried to teach me to swim. "On the third time down, you never come up," she

9

had said. Still, a small voice within told me, "Go down, do not attempt to swim!" I took a huge breath of air and headed for the murky bottom. When I reached the bottom, the voice said, "Go uphill!" It was easy to determine the right direction, and after taking a half-dozen steps, my head popped out into the air and I could breathe again. I walked out, dried off, put on my uniform and went back to camp. I never saw my so-called buddy again, but I learned one lesson that day: In this Army, do not trust anyone but yourself!

The next day I had to stand guard duty. I was issued a rifle and an MP armband, and told to report to Post Number 2 at 1800 hours.

At 2200, I was relieved and to my great surprise found that all MPs received free doughnuts and coffee at a special tent set up especially for those on guard duty. I saved my MP's armband, and every night thereafter went to the guard's tent at 2200 hours for free coffee and doughnuts. I never got assigned guard duty again; I guess they thought I was on duty every night.

The next day we all reported to the Pay Master for our monthly cash. I received my $21.00, which was standard for PFCs. I had some spare time and went down to the single hangar. The only plane in there was an old Stinson O-49, an observation high-wing monoplane. It also served as an air ambulance, using only one stretcher. One section of the hangar housed a meteorology station, including instrumentation for barometric pressure, temperature, wind direction and velocity and relative humidity measurements. I was unimpressed by the aircraft activity; there wasn't any.

About a week went by before I was called into the Captain's office. He advised me of my new rank, Staff Sergeant Pilot, U.S. Army Air Force. My pay would now be $196.00 a month, with fifty percent more for logging four hours of flying time. I sewed on the staff sergeant's insignia and went for a walk around camp, hoping I would run into our old drill corporal who had made my life so miserable.

Another week went by and once again I got called into the Captain's office. He had no special news, except to say, "We don't know what to do with you." He told me the Ferry Command may have a position open, or the Training Command may be in need of a flight instructor. His parting words were, "We know of nothing specific; I'll call you when something comes up."

After another month slipped by, I was again reporting to the Pay Master. Instead of $21.00, I received $196.00 in hard cash. I felt sorry for those stuck at $21.00. Another week passed, but not unnoticed. There was a line squall that knocked down many tents in

Tent City, where I was still billeted. Torrents of rain caused flash flooding of the camp and many duffle bags with precious contents went floating down Main Street towards the Gulf of Mexico.

The following day, the Captain called me back in and informed me that he had a request for Army glider pilots. He asked if I was interested. I replied, "I don't know what the U.S. AAF (Army Air Force) is coming to, but if they want me to fly baby carriages, that's OK with me—as long it has wings!"

My only previous encounter with gliders had been at the Taunton, Massachusetts, airport about two years earlier. I was ready for takeoff in my 40 hp Taylor Cub, and noticed a car towing a glider. When the glider got 100 feet off the ground, it cut loose and glided in for a landing 200 feet farther down the takeoff runway. What a joke, I thought. The flight lasted only a matter of seconds.

The Captain made the arrangements for cutting my new orders, assigning me to the U.S. Army Advanced Flying School at Elmira, New York. I was to travel by train, leaving Biloxi the next morning.

The author in his natural habitat: next to one of the many gliders he flew during the war

Chapter 3

LEARNING TO GLIDE

Elmira, New York

As the train pulled into the Elmira station, I wondered how I was to get to the U.S. AAF Advanced Flight School at Harris Hill. I did not have to wonder very long; after stepping off the train and walking along the old wooden platform, I saw an Army Weapons Carrier sitting in the station parking lot. A corporal sat at the wheel. As I approached, he said, "Sergeant, are you going to Harris Hill?" "Absolutely," I replied, "how do I get there?" He told me that Captain Langford had asked him to meet this train and pick up a staff sergeant that was coming in.

I reported to Captain Langford and he advised me that this was not a glider school, but an advanced sailplane flight school. We were the first class of twelve students, and we were to receive aeronautical courses at the Schweizer Aircraft Corporation factory. There would be classes on locating thermals and how to search them out, using an on-board instrument called a variometer. In addition, we would learn how to locate updrafts and downdrafts (and how to make efficient use of them), how to get the maximum distance when heading upwind or downwind and how to keep track of position in zero visibility. Next we would be given flight instruction in a sailplane and eventually graduate as glider pilots. We would then receive the silver wings with the letter "G" in the center.

Harris Hill was the sailplane center of the United States. The airfield was about 1,800 feet long by 800 feet wide. The hangar was located at the uphill end of the field. Most takeoffs were downwind and downhill. At the end of the takeoff run, the ground dropped 1,000 feet to the valley floor. Conversely, landings were always made uphill, regardless of the wind direction. When landing uphill into the wind, additional altitude is required to compensate for dangerous downdrafts, such as those on the approach to Harris Hill, which was situated on a cliff. Sailplanes caught in a downdraft without sufficient compensation had to abort their landings and revert to finding a suitable landing area in the valley below. Only occasionally could they catch a thermal and gain enough altitude for a second landing attempt at the hill.

On my first sailplane ride in a low-wing Schweizer, the instructor sat in the front seat, where the towline release was located. I was assigned to the rear seat, with limited visibility. This was to be an up-wind, downhill takeoff. The sailplane was parked near the hangar at the uphill end of the field, with its towline connected to the "D" plug in the tail of the tow plane. After we picked up our parachutes at the parachute tent, we headed for our glider. We did a pre-flight inspection of the aircraft, after which the instructor said, "OK, let's get in; put your chute in first, then get in and buckle up!"

"But I'd like to check my parachute first," I said.

He replied, "They are pre-inspected and are always OK." I told him that the wearer should always inspect a parachute before entering an aircraft. First, the flap that protects the ripcord should be opened, and the locking pins examined; they should never be bent or rusted. Second, the safety cord should be checked, to make sure it is intact. Lastly, the hand pull should be checked to see that it is in proper position, projecting out far enough from the pocket so that it is easily reachable if you need to use it.

Parachutes should be packed and repacked once every thirty days prior to being worn during aircraft flights, in accordance with Civil Air Regulation No. 25. I removed the card record from the parachute's card pocket and found it was over thirty days since this chute was packed. I told the instructor I'd like to go after another chute, if he didn't mind. After his OK, I picked up another chute and mentioned to him that a parachute is as a life vest to a drowning person. Take care of it, maintain it in proper condition, and when the time comes, you will be well repaid for your trouble.

We got in, put on our seat pack chutes and fastened our seat belts. The sailplane was equipped with wing skids to protect the wing tips from ground damage during landings. The landing gear on all Schweizer sailplanes consisted of a single wheel, located at the center of gravity, and a nose skid for short field landings. With this arrangement, takeoff required the assistance of a wing runner to hold the wing level until the glider reached an air speed of 20 mph, when aileron control was beginning to take over.

The wing runner was in position to lift the wing tip to the level position, which was the signal for the tow plane to start the takeoff run. As soon as the wings were leveled, and the slack came out of the 300-foot towline, rapid acceleration began. I felt pushed back into the seat. But the most surprising thing of all was the absolute silence of the takeoff, no usual roar of an aircraft engine. The instructor leveled off at ten feet above the tow plane and waited for his takeoff. As we approached the end of the field drop-off, the tow plane caught an updraft, which produced a 1,000 foot-per-minute rate of climb.

At 5,000 feet, the instructor climbed to fifty feet above the tow plane, nosed down, and when the towrope slackened, released the towline. Our excess speed was translated into additional altitude. The instructor said, "I'm going to do a series of lazy eights, then I want you to do them, OK?"

"OK," I said. I didn't know yet what the hell he was doing, but when he finished, I took over. I did my lazy eights like I always did them, and after several minutes I asked him if they were OK.

He replied, "Will you show me how to do that?"

"OK, I answered. "I'll explain."

The "lazy eight" is not one of those maneuvers in which the track of the entire glider describes a figure 8, but one in which the glider moves in only one general direction. The nose is made to swing up, down and sideways as though making a figure 8 on its side against the skyline. The glider is made to pitch and roll, like an ocean vessel quartering the wind in heavy seas.

For this maneuver, I selected an easily visible object on the ground several miles away, and not far below the horizon. In this case, I used a water tower as the point of intersection of the "8." Next, I headed the glider in a direction about 35° or 40° to one side of it. Then, I pulled the nose up to a steep climbing angle and, as it neared the peak of the climb, banked in toward the intersection point (the tower). I let the nose down again toward the point, and at such an angle that the nose appeared to cut the point (again, the tower) as it passed. I allowed the nose to continue in this direction until it was nearly the same distance off to the other side. Then, I took off the bank and pulled the nose up again. As I neared the steep climbing angle, I again banked toward the point and let the nose down as I passed it.

One flies this maneuver with a smooth, slow rhythm, without pausing in any part of it. In other words, the glider is continually changing its attitude in either climb, bank, glide or direction, and at times in three ways at once. It is impossible for any pilot to fly a perfect "lazy eight," unless he has mastered the Four Fundamentals of Flying: the climb, the bank, the turn and the straight and level.

The instructor took to this quickly, and did repeated it to the point where I thought I might become nauseated. He finally broke off the maneuver, and said, "We have just enough altitude to make it back to the hill. I want you to take over, land downwind uphill and make a series of S-turns in the updraft along the face of the landing area. I asked if I could use a side-slip on final. He said, "Try spoilers; they reduce lift by thirty percent, causing the glider to drop like an elevator. You can get your lift back by closing the spoilers just before touching down." As we approached the face of the landing field, we encountered strong updrafts all along the ridge. When we neared the right-hand side of the field, I made a 180° clockwise turn into the wind and applied drift angle compensation to maintain an equal distance from the face of the field. Upon reaching the left-hand side of the field, I made a counter-clockwise 180° turn, again using drift angle compensation to fly parallel to the face of the landing field. I discovered an amazing thing about the combined use of elevator and spoiler controls. In an updraft, these controls become interchangeable. The pilot can decide whichever is more comfortable for him.

While flying along this ridge, I used the spoilers to control altitude, while using the elevators for control of airspeed. I decided to interchange, using the elevators for control of altitude and spoilers for control of airspeed. This arrangement also worked, and was worth remembering.

The instructor asked, "Where did you learn how to do this?"

"Just now, right here!" I told him.

I landed along the right side of the field and after touchdown made a ground turn toward the hangar, the wing tip touching ground as the glider came to a stop close to the hangar. The instructor said, "That was a good approach and landing; what is your flying experience?" I told him that I learned to fly eight years earlier and had my own airport and flying school. The field was on a hill just like Harris Hill, where all landings were made uphill and takeoffs all downhill. He said, "Tomorrow you'll sit in the front seat on a solo flight. Look for thermals and see what you can do. Good luck!"

The next morning, reveille sounded at 0700. We enjoyed a delicious breakfast, just as we enjoyed every meal; they *all* seemed marvelous! It was like living in a luxurious private flying club, where everything was almost perfect. At 0800, assembly sounded and we all formed up in columns of four in the flagpole area, just downhill from the hangar.

The Commanding Officer, Captain Langford, also used this area to park his AT-6 advanced trainer, with a 600-plus horsepower air-cooled engine. Whenever a bogey aircraft appeared overhead, Langford would rush to his AT-6, jump in and give it full throttle downhill, taking off in hot pursuit. By the time he reached 5,000 feet, the bogey was long gone.

One time, a 1st lieutenant gave the order, "Attention!" and the squad snapped to it. As the color guard started to raise the flag, the lieutenant barked out his second order, "Present arms!" The squad responded with a snappy hand salute and held it there, awaiting the completion order. But that order was not forthcoming, as the lieutenant had forgotten what it was. He gave every order in the book to free us from our hand-held salute, but to no avail. Finally, another student arrived. He was a little late for assembly, and was an Officer in Grade at this glider training school. His name was Major Van Fleet. The lieutenant addressed him by asking, "Major, will you take over this squad?" Van Fleet stepped up ordering, "Order arms," and the squad completed the flag-raising salute. Then he went on his way; my guess was that he was exempt from close-order drill by any subordinate officer.

The lieutenant then barked another order, "Forward, march!"

As we moved out, I could see Langford's AT-6 directly ahead, but the lieutenant could not, because he was marching backwards. I could tell he was about to walk right up the tail section and put it out of service for at least a day. Sure enough, he stepped through the elevator fabric and fell directly on the rudder. The CO's plane was grounded!

At 1000 hours, I reported for flight duty. The tow plane and glider were connected by a standard 300-foot towline and were ready for takeoff. I inspected my parachute while the instructor was giving his last-minute flying advice.

"There are plenty of thermals breaking loose in the valley below; when one contacts your wing tip, it will lift the wing. Turn in that direction, making a 270° turn. Your variometer should register in the green, indicating an increase in the rate of climb. If it doesn't register, continue making 270° turns in a clover pattern, to seek out the maximum lift area. You're on your own. Good hunting!"

I took off downhill, downwind, and climbed up to a position ten feet above the tow plane. I leveled off and sustained that position until we reached 6,000 feet. When the tow plane flapped his wings, it signaled me to cut loose. I pulled up another thirty feet and dove toward the tow plane to pick up slack in the line, making it easier to operate the release mechanism. I then converted my excess speed into an additional 600 feet of altitude. The rushing sound of slipstream air reduced to a whisper. There was no engine noise; all was still and silent, except for the sound of a lonely train whistle far below. I had brought a box lunch and a pint of milk in a glass bottle, just in case I was forced down in some remote spot.

The thermals were easy to locate and I was able to fluctuate between 5,000 and 7,000 feet. At noon, I ate my lunch and finished the milk. But what was I to do with the bottle? I wanted to throw it out, but was concerned it might hit someone. If it remained with me, it might jam the controls if it got loose inside the glider's fuselage. I took another look around and saw nothing but trees, so out it went!

At 1300 hours, my position was about thirty miles SW of the field, and I felt it was time to go back. I reached the field around 1330, at 1,500 feet above the hill. I spent another hour flying the ridge, being careful not to get too close to the downdraft area on the downwind side. One of the other gliders had misjudged the lift area, ended up in the downdraft and was forced to land in the valley 1,000 feet below.

While I was still flying around the ridge, it started to rain. At first, it seemed like a shower, but a line squall developed. My glider was the highest of the four remaining gliders now also along the ridge. The lowest glider had the landing right-of-way. I would be last, all the while hoping I could control the glider until the others had landed. The first glider ended up on the downhill edge of the field. The second did a little bit better, landing at mid-field. The third also landed at mid-field. I analyzed the situation. They all expected to land uphill, downwind; but the line squall changed wind direction, which meant an uphill, upwind landing requiring more airspeed. I dropped the nose to obtain a 100-mph airspeed and came in low and fast. At mid-field, I noticed a man running uphill toward the hangar. He looked drenched; it was pouring rain! As I flew low past him, I thumbed my nose at him, because he was interfering with my landing pattern. I touched down and headed toward the open hangar door. By the time I reached the door, I was still going 20 mph. I continued into the hangar and applied the brake, so the ship came to rest in a nice dry hangar. The man who was running had by then reached the hangar. I hoped he did not recognize me, but he did. He said, "Nice landing, Bagley . . ." It was Major Van Fleet.

For the next three weeks, I spent my mornings attending aeronautical engineering classes at the Schweizer factory, while afternoons I practiced double and triple tows. The triple tow used a short 250-foot line, a medium line of 300 feet and a long line of 350 feet. This arrangement provided a fifty-foot clearance, horizontally, between the gliders during the tow period. After a while, the triple tow became boring and we had nothing to do except follow the tow plane. During our lunch period, the three of us who had just finished our third triple tow decided that on our next triple, we would "braid" the three towlines into a single strand. To accomplish this, the short line glider would move to the high tow position, and the other two gliders would then cross over. The short line glider would then move to the low tow position and again the other two gliders would cross over.

We were scheduled for our next triple tow the following day at 1200 hours. Just before takeoff, we confirmed our braiding idea. We flew in our standard tow positions until we reached 2,000 feet. The glider on the short towline went to the high position, allowing the others to cross over. The short line glider went to low tow, and the others again crossed over. We continued braiding until about 100 feet of towline was braided. At 4,000 feet, the tow signaled for us to cut loose. The tow plane headed back to the field, and we three gliders went our own way.

When I landed, my instructor was waiting for me at the hangar. I could sense he was serious when he said that we "had to talk." My guess was that he found out about our braiding and I was expecting a reprimand. I was surprised when he said, "We are transferring you to our instructors' class. Tomorrow you will begin instructing glider pilots; meet me in the instructors' lounge at 0900 sharp!"

The next morning I reported and was introduced as the new instructor. I was told that my first student was ready for spins, that his elementary flying was satisfactory. The ground crew had parked the glider in the takeoff area and connected a 350-foot towline. My new student was halfway through the pre-flight inspection when I arrived. I introduced myself, and then completed the pre-flight inspection of both glider and parachute. I was in the rear seat and found the visibility to be almost blind. I hoped he could handle the takeoff, because I could not even see the tow plane as we started our takeoff roll. I told him to climb to ten feet above the tow plane and hold that relative position. We finally got the signal to cut free at 6,000 feet. I advised my student to climb to fifty feet above the tow plane, then nose down to pick up slack in the towline, release, then use the excess speed to gain additional altitude. He followed the instruction to the letter. I advised him that we were to practice a few spins. My suggestion was met with an enthusiastic "OK!"

I told him, "I'm going to do a two-turn spin to the right. I want you to follow through on the controls, to get the feel of them as we go through this maneuver." I told him it was essential that every student know how to spin and recover before soloing, because it not only gives you confidence in your ability, but helps to develop a better technique in handling the glider. I told him he would soon see that a tailspin is not nearly as dangerous as one might think.

I advised him that before trying this maneuver, he must look carefully for other aircraft beneath him. One way to go into a spin is to pull the nose up slightly, while keeping the wings level, then wait for the glider to lose speed. As it approaches a stall, apply full rudder in the direction you want to spin. Then pull the stick all the way back, evenly, using no aileron.

To come out of the spin, place the rudder in a neutral position and push the stick gently ahead, until the spin is definitely broken. Then pull up from the dive smoothly and evenly, so that the nose is as near to the horizon as it was when you started.

I told my student, "I will now make a two-turn, right-hand spin. Are you ready?" The student said, "Yeah, I'll follow through!" I made the spin, then asked him to do a two-turn spin to the right, completely on his own. Again he agreed. His spin was satisfactory, but it was two and one-half turns, not two. I asked that he do another, suggesting that he look at the ground while spinning in order to keep oriented. I told him always to start a spin into the wind, facing a designated spot on the horizon. To stop the spin completely, pull the nose straight up to the same pre-designated spot.

On the second spin, he headed into the wind, selected a point on the horizon and began. But he never finished it; after three or more tries he became nauseous, heaving his breakfast all over the front cockpit, including the windshield. As a result, I couldn't see a damn thing, except from the two small windows on either side of the floor. I leveled it off at about 1,500 feet and headed for Harris Hill. We made it back to the field, landed and turned the glider over to the ground crew for a thorough cleanup. The student asked me bluntly if I was going to wash him out because of his airsickness. I replied that I did not have that authority, that all I could do was to make a recommendation. I told him I did not feel that his airsickness would be a problem. As an instructor, I have become nauseated while a student was flying. The person doing the flying rarely becomes sick; it is most always the one who isn't at the controls. I told him that on our next flight, we would test my theory. He was to do all the flying, from takeoff to landing. I said I felt that my two spins were the cause of his airsickness; at least it may have started the queasy sensation.

The next morning we took off once again, with my student in the pilot's seat. I told him we were up there for one reason only: to demonstrate his ability to enter into the tailspin maneuver and make a safe recovery from it. At 5,000 feet, the tow plane signaled to cut off. After that, the student nosed up and approached stalling speed. Using full left rudder, he brought the stick all the way back, and the glider started a left-hand spin. After two turns, the student neutralized the rudder and moved the stick forward slightly. The spin was broken. He returned to normal level flight. I told him, "That's it for today; let's get back to Harris Hill and land."

After landing, I told him what my report would say: "The student has a tendency to become nauseated, but in spite of the feeling was able to demonstrate his ability to enter into a tailspin and make a safe recovery." Relieved, he gushed, "Hey, thanks!" I told him that he earned it. No pilot who has ever experienced nausea while flying would wash him out. I then advised him that we would be going on a special flight in the morning and that I would review the details with him on the flight line at 0900.

The weather next morning was 100 percent overcast, with stratus clouds at 2,000 feet. I met my student at 0900 sharp, with our glider and tow plane standing by. I explained this was to be a cross-country flight of thirty miles. Meanwhile, Captain Langford took off in his AT-6 to investigate the depth of the clouds and the possibility of climbing above the cloud layer. He landed fifteen minutes later and reported that the stratus cloud layer was about 1,000 feet thick, but he ran into clear skies at about 3,000; he thought it would burn off in a few hours.

The tow plane pilot and Captain Langford held a private conference and decided to go through with the cross-country flight. I told my student that he was to do all the flying. We took off at 0930 and headed west. I told him to keep track of our headings during the tow, because we would have to get above the overcast if we wanted to be able find our way back. The tow plane flew on its southerly heading for about five minutes before we ascended into the stratus clouds. We then lost sight of our tow plane and the horizon. It was difficult for us to stay in our proper place, which was ten feet above the tow plane, to avoid the turbulence produced by its prop.

I instructed the student to observe the angle between the towline and our longitudinal centerline. I told him to maintain the same angle during periods when the tow plane was not visible. If that angle becomes more obtuse, the glider is too high; if more acute, the glider is too low.

After three minutes on this heading, we burst through the overcast into clear sunny skies, just as Captain Langford predicted. The tow plane then turned north, and held that heading for ten minutes. We received the cut off signal at 5,000 feet. The student cut off in the usual manner and gained an additional 300 feet in altitude. The overcast clouds were 2,500 feet below; we saw no evidence of any thermals, which usually break up and shred the stratus blanket.

I asked my student to give me the heading for Harris Hill. His reply was, "The compass heading is ninety degrees." I then asked him for the wind direction. He stated, "East wind, at 20 mph." I directed him to establish a return heading of 135° and advised that we had a cross headwind from our left. I let him know we had a long flight and would be lucky to make Harris Hill. Flying into a headwind requires greater airspeed. Greater airspeed can only be obtained by sacrificing altitude. Instead of cruising at 60 mph, I told him to cruise at 80 mph, continuing at that speed and present compass heading until he could see the horizon at the bottom of the overcast. Before letting down through the cloud layer, I instructed him to take his hands and feet completely off the controls and observe the attitude of the glider. He did as I requested and, noticing that the glider remained in stable flight, continued on the same heading and airspeed. This meant we had properly adjusted the trim tabs for hands-off flying. Because we were about to enter the stratus layer, I asked him to take over the controls again and begin our letdown through 1,000 feet of blind, zero visibility in barely-able-to-see-our-wing-tips conditions.

My experience taught me that if you find your airspeed increasing, and easing back on the stick to slow down causes an increase in airspeed, it means that you are in a downward spiral and your controls are not responding as expected. Without blind flying instruments, we have no way of knowing the attitude of the glider;

the best thing to do is go to hands-off control and allow the glider to stabilize itself.

The student experienced no difficulty in performing the blind flying let-down. Our horizon was re-established at 2,000 feet, with visibility at twenty miles. Harris Hill was visible three miles ahead, but we were only 1,000 feet above the field with a glide ratio[1] of twelve or fourteen to one. Several gliders were visible on final approach and were landing uphill, upwind. We continued on our present heading until we were tangential to the landing field, then made a 90° left turn onto our final landing pattern. We now had a tailwind and I requested airspeed of 40 mph to conserve altitude. We found ourselves at a distance of 1,000 feet from our landing area, but 100 feet below it. We were still losing altitude.

The student asked nervously, "What do we do now?"

I said, "Just keep the same airspeed and heading. When we get within 500 feet of the cliff, make a 90° right turn and fly parallel to it. We should run into updrafts any second." Just as the student made the 90° turn, we ran into a strong updraft. Our variometer went into its full-scale green reading. I asked my student pilot to make a series of S-turns along the face of the cliff, until we had gained an altitude of 400 feet above our landing area. Then I had him use full spoilers for a downwind, uphill landing. He made a good landing, taxied up to the hangar area and applied the brake as the wing tip touched down. We were both glad to be back.

After dinner, an announcement came over the PA system that all personnel were to meet in the Assembly Room at 1900 hours. We were told that as of 0900 the next day, we all would receive our graduation diplomas. We were then to report to the Orderly Room and pick up our orders for our next assignment. That evening, I packed my meager possessions in my duffle bag and was ready to move at a moment's notice.

At 0900 hours, assembly sounded and we all got into formation at the flagpole area. There were several newspaper reporters with cameras ready to roll. Captain Langford called the name of each graduate, starting with the instructors' class. When my name came up, I marched up to the Captain and received my diploma. I saluted him and returned to the order. The news cameras were cranking away, while reporters asked questions and interviewed graduates.

---

[1] The distance that is traveled through the air per each foot of altitude lost; e.g., if during the time the glider has dropped ten feet, a distance of 100 miles was traveled, the glide ratio is 10:1.

After the ceremony, I reported to the Orderly Room for my new assignment.

The order stated that I was to report to the Advanced Glider School in Lockbourne, Ohio, as a Flight Instructor. I was authorized to travel POC, or by "Privately Owned Conveyance." Another instructor, Bill Dickson, was also assigned to the same unit, and we decided to travel together since we had the same authorization. Traveling POC implied one had a car and would be reimbursed for mileage. Since neither of us had a car, we decided to hitchhike and keep track of the mileage.

Lockbourne was located ten miles south of Columbus, Ohio. We left Elmira in early July 1942, and started our 400-mile trek.

Chapter 4

ADVANCED GLIDER SCHOOL
Columbus, Ohio

I t took Dickson and me three days to hitch from Elmira, New York to Columbus, Ohio. Travel by automobile was very slow due to a 35 mph speed limit imposed to conserve fuel and reduce tire wear. Tires constructed using inner tubes were unreliable, especially when the tubes were installed in a damaged tire. And new tires were about as scarce as hen's teeth!

We arrived in Columbus about noon and after lunch, Dickson decided to purchase a used car. We located a used car lot and found a 1939 Chevrolet sedan that was to Dickson's liking. He went into the office, got the keys and we gave it a test drive. It took fast-talking Dickson about an hour to negotiate with the dealer and leave holding the keys.

About a half-hour later, we arrived at the Lockbourne U.S. Army Air Forces Base. The guard at the gate gave us directions to the administrative office, where we reported to the Commanding Officer. The CO welcomed us and advised that we would be flying a variety of sailplanes and gliders using single, double and triple tows. We had only a single runway, which had just been completed, and our second runway was still under construction. The CO called in his Master Sergeant and told him to handle our settling-in paperwork. The Sergeant escorted us to his office and began sorting out various forms and applications. He advised us that the rank of Staff Sergeant allowed married couples to live off base. Married couples were also given an allowance for food and housing. Dickson advised him that he was married and wanted authorization to live outside the base.

The Master Sergeant turned to me and said, "I suppose you want to live off base also?"

I replied, "Definitely."

He then asked, "What is your wife's name?"

"Mary."

"Where is she now?"

"Hollywood."

"What is the address?" I told him.

"Telephone number?" I told him that, too.

"Why isn't she with you?

"I have to find a place to live first."

He handed me the completed authorization form for my signature. I signed the form and handed it back. After completing Dickson's form, he authorized two days to locate apartments. We were to report on the flight line at 0900 sharp on the third day.

Dickson and I drove back to Columbus to hunt for apartments. I was lucky; I found a wonderful three-room one, fully furnished, for $60 a month.

That evening I called Mary and asked her if she would like to get married. I told her that I had already rented an apartment and was assigned to Lockbourne as a flight instructor. I told her that I would call her tomorrow for the answer. We had previously talked about marriage, but were not sure whether we should get married sooner or later. It's impossible to know your fate in time of war.

When I called her back the next day, she said she had purchased her railroad tickets and would arrive in Columbus in three days.

Dickson found an apartment close by, and since we both had the same schedule, I arranged for him to provide transportation for me to and from the base. I agreed to pay him something each week for this service.

When we reported to the flight line, we were given specific assignments. I was asked to report to a 1st lieutenant, who was standing by an AT-6 tow plane.

"Sergeant," he said, "we have to pick up a Wolf glider in Akron, Ohio that has been assigned to this base." I picked up a parachute and climbed into the front seat. He had the 300-foot towline packed into the baggage compartment. After warming up the engine and checking both magnetos, oil pressure, RPM, manifold pressure and temperature, we taxied to the holding area at one end of the only active runway. We had to wait for several glider takeoffs, but finally were cleared.

The 600-plus horsepower radial came to life with a tremendous roar, the propeller blades set in low pitch for rapid acceleration. We took off into an overcast sky, on a 40° heading to Akron, Ohio. Thirty minutes later, we spotted the airport approximately five miles ahead. The lieutenant picked up the mike and said, "This is Army AT-6 at 5,000 feet, request landing instructions, over."

"This is Akron tower. Land runway 18, wind velocity NNW at 5, altimeter 29.92, traffic pattern is right hand; call on downwind leg. Over."

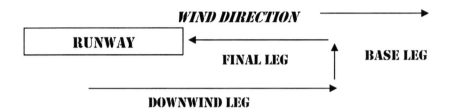

Two minutes later we turned into our downwind leg, and the Lieutenant again picked up the mike. "AT-6 to Akron tower; we are turning downwind, over."

"Roger; you are number one to land, runway 18."

The Lieutenant cranked down ten degrees of flaps and made a perfect three-point landing. We spotted our Wolf glider parked opposite the hangar.

Then we heard, "Tower to Navy F4U Corsair; you are cleared for takeoff runway 18 as soon as the AT-6 is clear of the runway."

Just after turning on to the taxi strip, the Corsair went roaring by in low pitch and full power right out of their factory. We taxied over to the hangar and parked on the apron. The Lieutenant thinned out the fuel-air ratio, shut down the engine, waited for the propeller to stop rotating and then turned off the switch. We climbed out of the airplane and noticed a captain walking toward us from the open hangar door. We introduced ourselves, and he informed us that he was the Procurement Officer for South East Air Force Training Command, responsible for transferring the Wolf glider to Lockbourne. He asked if I had ever flown a Wolf glider. "Never," I said.

He replied, "Well, it has a poor glide ratio when compared to sailplanes, and . . . we have another problem."

Curious, I asked, "What?" He said, "The hatch cover and wind screen is all in one piece; it's not hinged or permanently attached— it's removable. After the pilot gets in, the hatch cover is placed in position and secured by two screen-door-type sliding bolts located on the inside. They're operated by the pilot. Last month, one of our pilots was flying a Wolf when the hatch came off, giving the pilot a rabbit punch to the back of the neck, killing him. I thought you should know."

"Thanks," I said. "I'll give it a good pre-flight inspection."

The Lieutenant signed for the glider, after which the ground crew lined it up with its towline on the edge of the runway. He then taxied the AT-6 into position. The ground crew connected the towline to the "D" plug in the tail, then signaled we were ready for takeoff. Acceleration was rapid, and the Wolf was airborne at 60 mph, about 400 feet down the 5,000-foot runway. The AT-6 was still on the runway. When my airspeed reached 85 mph, the AT-6 became airborne; by the end of the runway, we were cruising at 120 mph at 1,000 feet. The glider was redlined at 120 mph, which meant it was not safe to exceed that airspeed.

We leveled off at 5,000 feet. The sky grew increasingly overcast and the air temperature was dropping, indicating the approach of a rapid-moving cold front. It started to rain; the air became turbulent. The tow plane was bouncing around like a cork. As the rain and turbulence increased, the sound increased proportionately to where it sounded like I was inside a bass drum. I realized we were in the center of a line squall. We were told in our meteorology class that there was always a twenty-mile section along every cold front that was extremely violent and within which aircraft could not survive. The hatch was vibrating violently, which sounded like the rumbling of a freight train. I remembered what the Procurement Officer told me about the hatch killing the pilot as it flew off. My reaction was to get away from it, but that was not possible at that moment. The best I could do was lean as far forward as possible, and keep my head down. I got down without losing sight of the tow plane, wondering if the hatch would fly off.

With a loud bang, followed by a thud that shook the whole glider, the hatch was gone. The thud was caused by the hatch bumping the vertical fin. I looked over my shoulder, but could see no damage; the fin was still there. I could no longer see the tow plane because the rain hitting my eyes at 120 mph was too painful! The windscreen hatch was gone and I had no helmet or goggles for protection; the rain was very heavy and my face felt the sting of every drop. The only solution was to put my hand over my eyes and look through the cracks between my fingers to bring the tow plane into view.

After ten minutes of finger-crack flying, I wondered if my parachute was still safe to use. I decided it was not, due to the complete drenching it received after the hatch flew off. I prayed that the towline would not break. It would leave me at 5,000 feet with zero visibility and no parachute! I asked myself, what would I do then? The only thing left would be to slow the glider to its absolute minimum air speed and, when it fell off to the left or right, use rudder to compensate. This is called "walking it down."

My prayers must have been answered, because we broke out into a clear blue sky with the air base in plain sight. About five miles from the field, I cut loose from the tow plane, still shielding my eyes from the rushing air. I wanted to reduce speed to 40 mph, because then I could uncover my eyes. I knew the tow plane pilot would fly on. After dropping the towrope on the apron, he would advise the tower of a glider in free flight approaching the runway from the northeast.

Arriving over the air base, I observed several gliders, tow planes and ground crews gathered at one end of the runway. There were several gliders in free flight. To save time and avoid traffic congestion, I decided to land on a taxi strip leading up to the hangar. I parked near the hangar and advised the ground crew to give the Wolf a thorough inspection.

The next morning, I went down to the flight line to find the Wolf ready for flight. After cadets completed their first solo, they were allowed to fly the single-seat gliders. The instructor was giving the cadet sitting in the Wolf final landing pattern instructions, after which the cadet asked, "How does this fly, compared to a Schweizer?"

The instructor replied, "Like a brick."

For safety, the pilot was assigned helmet and goggles and the tow plane pilots were restricted to 70 mph when towing the Wolf. I watched as they took off and climbed to 5,000 feet. Just south of the field, the glider cut loose. The tow plane went into a steep dive. He dropped his rope, made a 270° turn and was making a wheel landing on the runway. Out of nowhere came the Wolf, also making a wheel landing on the same runway at a greater speed. The glider passed the tow plane by going under his wing and was barely able to stop before running out of runway.

In the meantime, the lieutenant who flew the tow plane on our ferry trip from Akron walked up to me and handed me the hatch that flew off during our flight. He said, "Look, I found it!"

"Thanks," I said, and took it to a flat spot on the apron. I carefully laid it on the tarmac and jumped on it until it was completely destroyed. "That probably saved someone's life," I told him.

When I arrived back at the apartment, I found a telegram from Mary. It said she would be arriving the next day on the 12:30 p.m. train. I called the base and got the day off. First thing in the morning, I purchased a gently used 1939 Plymouth sedan for $200. At least now we would be self-sufficient.

Mary looked stunning as she stepped off the train. We had been apart only a few months, but it felt like an eternity to me. We had lunch, then went to our apartment, which really impressed her.

Getting married wasn't easy; we had to make applications and get blood tests. I was Catholic and wanted to be married in the Church, or at least by a priest. Mary was not a Catholic, but agreed to be married by a priest.

We went to the rectory and managed to meet with a priest who made the necessary arrangements. We set a date for our wedding: August 2, 1942.

On that day, we went to the rectory and asked for Father John. As soon as he entered the office, I asked if he could marry us that day, as soon as possible.

"Oh, no . . ." he said, telling us we had to wait for an approval. I advised him that we had complied with all the requirements and if he could not marry us right then, we were going downtown to the Justice of the Peace, because today we were getting married! He called various workers and maids together, performed the ceremony and pronounced us man and wife.

That afternoon I called the air base and spoke to Flight Operations to see what my schedule called for. I was scheduled for night flying that very night. I attempted to talk my way out of it, but to no avail. It was my wedding night and I had to spend it flying instead of with my new bride!

It happened to be the first time for night flying at this base, so there was no way I was getting out of it. The Operations Officer gave the overall flight plan: "The runway is 5,000 feet long, but we will be using only 4,000 feet. It will be lighted by smudge pots at 200-foot intervals, since electric power is not available for the regular runway lights."

After takeoff, each glider was to proceed to Zone Red at 6,000 feet altitude, north of the base. When the glider had descended to an altitude of 4,000 feet, it was to proceed to Zone Yellow, west of the base. When the glider descended to 2,000 feet, it would enter the Green Zone, and from there enter the base leg for final approach to the runway.

"Any questions?" There was no response.

We took off and soon found ourselves at 2,000 feet in the Green Zone. Oddly, the tow plane pilot signaled for us to cut loose. The student was flying from the front seat and I instructed him to do so.

"But, Sir," he said, "we're not in the proper zone!"

"Cut loose, he must be in trouble!" I insisted. As soon as we cut loose, the tow plane headed straight down, diving toward the runway. I saw his plane touch down in a fast wheel landing, just as he came into the dim light produced by the smudge pots. His plane was still rolling down the runway, 1,000 feet from where he first touched down.

The plane slowed and the pilot jumped from it. He ran to the edge of the runway and disappeared into the darkness between the smudge pots. Then it happened–the whole runway burst into flames, including the plane, which was still rolling. The flames were fifty feet high and burned all along the runway; the tow plane exploded, sending flaming fuel in all directions.

Now the question was, what the hell were we going to do? We had no place to land—the only runway was on fire and there was nothing but blackness all around.

I knew that the new runway was not usable due to construction activity. I also knew its centerline was 90° from the approach to our burning runway. I decided if we came into the burning runway on our final leg, and made a 45° turn to the right, we would land in the grassy area between the two runways. I instructed the student to make a standard approach to the burning runway and told him I would advise him when to make a 45° turn to the right. "OK!" he said tensely.

I told him, "After you make the 45° turn, slow the glider to 40 mph. Apply full spoilers, and wait for the wheel to touch down. Push the stick all the way forward to put the glider on its nose shield for a short field landing."

As we approached the runway, I said, "Make your 45° right turn now!" He did, and thankfully everything worked out as I had expected. I told my student, "This is my honeymoon and I'm getting out of here. I'll see you tomorrow."

Mary and I celebrated our first wedding night with a bottle of champagne at midnight.

The next day, ground crews moved our glider to the apron area. They told us that if we had continued for another 500 feet, we would have run into a steamroller that had parked in that open area! After all, the second runway was still under construction.

I located our tow plane pilot and asked him what happened. He said that after takeoff, he climbed to 2,000 feet and noticed that the fuel was down by a quarter of a tank. His fuel level was going down fast, so he signaled us to release the towline. He jumped out of the plane as it continued to roll because he knew that when the fuel gushing from the ruptured tank encountered a flame from one of the many smudge pots, all hell would break loose! He used his head and saved his life.

Night flying continued for another two weeks, after which the class graduated. We were assigned a new group of cadets for basic and advanced flying. My student, Cadet June, and I took off in a TG-2 Schweizer. We were about five miles south of our base when the towline snapped. I asked June to release what was left of the towline, to prevent it from catching on a solid object during our landing. There were no thermals and we had insufficient altitude to make it back to base.

"June, you have the controls; pick a field and land," I said.

His choice was excellent. The field was long and wide. It looked like a hay field, flat and green. Along one side of the field was a row of fence posts. June lined the glider up for the landing and established a constant glide. His airspeed was 60 mph, making a straight-in approach. I asked him where exactly he was going to touch down, if he held the current airspeed and altitude.

"I don't know," he said.

"Exactly in the center at mid-field," I explained.

"How can you be sure?" he asked. I asked him to observe the fence posts at the beginning of the field, compare them to the fence posts at the far end of the field and to tell me the difference.

"They look the same," he said, "except they get smaller with distance."

"Look at the distance between the fence posts at the end of the field and tell me what you see."

"Oh!" he said, after close observation, "the fence posts at this end are getting farther apart."

"Yes, and what about those at the far end?"

"They are getting closer together."

"That's right," I said. "Those that are getting farther apart are the ones you will pass over and those that are getting closer together you will not pass over. But the ones that are stationary, not getting farther apart or closer together, mark the spot at which the glider will touch down."

The place of no movement; this is exactly how an outfielder is able to catch that high fly ball. He runs in the direction in which the ball is moving and when he gets to the spot where the ball is not moving, he knows that the ball will drop right into his glove. That same point at mid-field would be our touchdown point.

I added, "If you want to land sooner simply apply spoilers and observe where that null point is located; it will be closer."

June used spoilers and landed in the beginning one-third of our selected field.

The tow plane arrived about twenty minutes later and dropped a new towline. We moved the glider to one side of the field, allowing the tow plane to make an unobstructed landing. There was sufficient headwind so we used the aileron control to pick up the wing resting on its skid to a level position—the signal for the tow plane to start take off. Soon we were on our way. We saved the ground crew a trip and having to disassemble the glider and trailer it back to base, usually requiring two days out of service.

A couple of days later, June and I were again flying. Just after takeoff, at 200 feet, the towline ruptured. "I'll take it," I said. We were over a huge cornfield adjacent to the air base; the rows of corn were directly ahead. I decided to try and land between the rows, which were a little wider than the width of the fuselage. I slowed to 40 mph, let the glider contact the tops of the corn and eased back on the stick to stay airborne longer. It was a very soft landing; we never even felt the wheel make ground contact.

After stopping, I got out onto the wing and stepped off. It was a hell of a step; the glider was, in fact, four feet off the ground, supported entirely by the corn! June got out, sat on the wing and eased himself down. The corn was at least six feet tall and saturated with dew. By the time we worked our way out of that field, we were soaked. We went to Operations and told them of our mishap. The Air Force had to send a Damage Control Officer to estimate the extent of the crop damage, including the damage that would now result from sending in a ground crew with equipment, trucks and trailers. They needed to cut a road through the cornfield to gain access to the glider. The farmer was paid $600 for estimated crop damage. He was delighted and wondered how often this might happen. I told him we would try to land on the same spot next time, to minimize the damage!

That evening, Dickson dropped me off at home, and I found that Mary had fixed t-bone steaks for dinner, one of my favorites. She was upbeat, singing songs from the movie *Me and My Gal*, a picture she had just finished at MGM Studios, where she was under contract. After dinner, Mary announced that she had some great news. She had found a lovely apartment nearby, smaller, but for half the rent. I told her if she was happy with it, it was OK with me. We moved over the weekend.

❖   ❖   ❖

Monday morning, when Dickson and I arrived at the flight line, we came upon an unbelievable scene. Three gliders—one Schweizer, one Pratt-Reed and one Wolf—were all hanging by their noses from the tail of an O-49 Stinson, which was at 400 feet. The O-49 tow plane was flying at thirty mph, while the tail of the Wolf hung fifty feet above the ground. Its air-cooled radial engine was at full throttle, with the prop set in low pitch making a tremendous roar. The tow plane pilot was guiding the three vertically dangling gliders over flat areas to avoid buildings, hangars and other structures. I could see he was gaining a little altitude, perhaps at the rate of two or three feet per minute. What must the pilots on board those gliders be thinking? They would all be killed if the triple towrope supporting all three gliders gave way and they ended up in a heap on the tarmac! Or, if the towline broke on the highest glider, it would plummet downward into the other two below, causing all three to go down. The two upper gliders had students and instructors on board; the Wolf, a single-seater, was piloted by a student. I hoped that he would not sacrifice himself to save the other four.

On the other hand, if he did release, the tow plane could recover air speed and altitude, and possibly restore normal level flight to the remaining gliders. All we could do was watch and get the ambulance crew and medics to stand by for the worst-case scenario. We hoped the O-49's engine would not fail. The instructor in the glider just above the student in the Wolf was giving instructions to him. We could hear them talking, but could not distinguish the words because of the roaring, flat pitch of the O-49's propeller. After twenty minutes into this critical situation, the tow plane gained another fifty feet. Time seemed to stand still. The Wolf glider now had 100 feet of altitude, still not enough to recover from a whipstall[2] in the event of release. At the present rate of climb, the Wolf glider's tail section would be at a safe release altitude for a whipstall recovery in twenty-eight minutes. Could the O-49 hold out mechanically? The tow plane pilot could decide to let them all down gradually in the grassy area between the runways or when all three gliders were on the ground, the tow plane could release the triple towline. But in this situation, the tow plane itself would be at risk of stalling out and crashing on top of the released gliders.

All we could do was wait and hope none of the pilots made a drastic mistake. It seemed like an eternity, but after the twenty-eight minutes passed, the tow plane had gained another 700 feet. The tail section of the Wolf was now 800 feet above the tarmac, which was sufficient for a safe release and recovery from a whipstall.

The tow plane was moving toward the grassy area between our two runways, when the Wolf pilot released his towline. In a fraction of a second, the Wolf whipped smartly back and down, accelerating at the rate of thirty-two feet per second. Amazingly, the pilot was able to make a full recovery and returned to normal flight at 100 feet, landing in the grassy area.

The Pratt-Reed was the next to release, followed by the Schweizer. Astonishingly, they too made perfect landings. The tow plane dropped the triple towrope, landed and taxied to the hangar apron area. He was met by the Commanding Officer of the base. After some discussion, the CO advised the pilot that he was bringing court martial charges against him for flying while intoxicated.

Later that day, I went to the base headquarters office and asked to see the CO. After a ten-minute wait, the orderly came over and said, "He will see you now."

---

[2] A steep climb that causes the glider to stall. Characterized by a violent, backwards then downward "whipping" motion. To perform this as a flying maneuver, the glider must be nosed down at 140-150 mph and the elevator column pulled back abruptly. The elevator control column should be kept all the way back until an airspeed of 80 mph is reached. Then the pilot can make a "recovery" and return to level flight.

As I walked in, the CO put me at ease and asked what he could do for me. I told him it was concerning the tow plane pilot that was to be court-martialed for flying drunk. "Continue," he said. Regarding the pilot, I told him, "Even though he was drunk, he was able to demonstrate excellent flying ability. He didn't panic or cause injury to those involved." I went on to say that I doubted any pilot who witnessed that precarious event could do a better job. Besides, I didn't think it was all his fault. The O-49 was not powerful enough to handle a triple tow; it took at least an AT-6 with its 600-plus horsepower radial. The O-49 should be regulated to only double or single tows.

"That's it, Sir," I said. "I thought you should know." The CO thanked me, saying, "I'll take it under consideration." I thanked him, saluted and left his office. I don't know anything more about the court martial, but the O-49s were soon restricted to single or double tows.

❖   ❖   ❖

Mary's eighteen-year-old brother, John W. Walsh, came for a two-day visit. He was also under contract with MGM Studios, playing the part of a Spitfire[3] pilot during the Battle of Britain in the movie *Eagle Squadron.* Previously, he had played a part in *Boys' Town,* with Spencer Tracy playing the part of Father Flanagan. John was in the final scene, coming into Boys' Town with his dog, limping all the way. The director later complimented John on his limp; "It looked real," he said. John replied, "It was real . . . I sprained my ankle last night!"

John and I went to the base to observe the activities. He felt that if drafted, his preference would be the Air Force and he wanted a firsthand look at what was involved. Since I was not scheduled for flight duty, I decided to fly the *Minamoa,* a German-built, gull-wing sailplane with the highest glide ratio of any sailplane of its day. The pilot practically had to lie down in very cramped quarters, due to its efficient design and low lift-to-drag ratio. It had a landing gear, but it was never used for landings, only for takeoffs.

As soon as the glider was airborne, the landing gear was jettisoned by pulling the gear release ring on the floor. All landings were made on wood belly skis. This was a single-seat sailplane, reserved for instructors only as it was the only existing flyable one in the U.S. It

---

[3] The Spitfire *Supermarine* was a British single-seat fighter plane, known by pilots for its ease in handling.

was indeed a privilege to fly such a famous sailplane. The *Minamoa* had broken many records for endurance, altitude and cross-country flights.

After pre-flighting the glider, I adjusted my parachute, got in, fastened the seat belt, and secured the hatch. The ground crew connected the towline to the AT-6, and I gave the signal for takeoff. The glider accelerated rapidly and was airborne in less than 100 feet. The tow plane was still on the ground when I released the landing gear. As we gained altitude, I saw a strange sight. My pair of wheels was racing down the runway! The glider was quiet, compared to the regular training gliders, even at 120 mph. I cut loose at 5,000 feet, picked up a thermal, and gained another 2,000 feet. The glider was very sensitive and responsive to all control movements.

After a half-hour of various maneuvers, lazy eights, wing-overs and split S-turns, I decided to land on runway 18. I was on final approach, at an altitude of 500 feet. The distance to the runway was 1600 feet, with the runway dead center ahead. I passed over the end of the runway at ten feet with an airspeed of 60 mph and waited for the glider to slow. Instead, the airspeed was increasing rapidly. Halfway down the 5,000-foot runway, the airspeed reached 100 mph—without a tow plane! When I reached the far end of the runway, the airspeed was 120 mph. Since the wind velocity was less than 4 or 5 mph, I made an Immelman turn[4], heading north at 1,000 feet, with an air speed of 60 mph. This was my *new* downwind leg for a landing on runway 18. I turned to base and then final for a second landing attempt. The same thing happened again; the airspeed went to 120 mph and I made another Immelman turn heading north. I concluded this glider was not going to come down, at least not on the runway.

The runway was acting like a thermal generator. It was a sunny day with no wind and the cement runway was hot, a combination of physical variables that prevented the high performance sailplane from landing. I could see now why the landing gear was disposable; if a wheel landing were attempted without brakes, the glider would run

---

[4] To perform this maneuver, airspeed must be increased to 140-150 mph. Then the glider is pulled up into the first half of a loop. When the glider is upside-down, the control column is pushed forward and to one corner. At the same time, full opposite rudder is applied. As the glider rolls toward an even keel, the control column is pulled back and across to the opposite corner, while full opposite rudder is applied. This will stop any further rotation. As the glider levels off, the rudder must be straightened and the control column pushed forward until cruising airspeed is reached. This maneuver is used to change direction with a minimum loss of altitude. Simply put, the glider is pulled into a half-loop, with a rollover at the top.

out of runway and crash. Moreover, the additional combined weight of a fixed landing gear and brakes would have greatly reduced its efficiency.

There was a grassy area running parallel to runway 18, which was my choice for a third landing attempt. The airspeed on final was 60 mph with an altitude of fifteen feet at the beginning of the grassy area, which extended for 5,000 feet. I maintained an airspeed of 60 mph until the landing skid contacted the grass at about mid-runway, when rapid deceleration began. The glider skidded to a stop 600 feet from the point of touchdown. I opened the hatch and got out, just as the ground crew approached with the jettisoned landing gear. They re-attached the wheels and we moved the glider back to the flight line where John had been waiting. He had been observing various glider activities in progress and was impressed with the performance of the *Minamoa.*

That evening, Mary, John and I went out for dinner in celebration of John's visit. He was scheduled to leave the next morning to visit relatives in New England before returning to California.

The following day I was scheduled to fly with three students. The first was a captain who was receiving flight instruction as an in-grade officer. He was difficult, not because he was a captain, but because he could not master the four fundamentals of flying. He absolutely could not catch on to straight and level flying. His left wing was always low; as a result, his left-hand turns were all slipping turns and all his right hand turns, skidding turns. After a week of trying to correct the problem, I gave up and requested that prior to washout, he be assigned to another instructor for a second opinion.

The second student was very good in all aspects of flying, and I decided to teach him a Falling Leaf maneuver. It is decidedly spectacular to watch as the glider flutters silently toward the ground. We took off in a TG-2 Schweizer, climbed to 7,000 feet and released from our tow plane.

My instructions to the student were as follows: "For this maneuver, pull the stick straight back, and as the glider stalls, apply full right rudder. The right wing will start to drop, as in the first stage of a spin. But before the spin gets under way, apply full left rudder. The glider now swings over to the left and attempts to spin in this direction, but the spin is again prevented by application of full right rudder. The left wing comes up, the glider swings over and the right wing is down again. Seesawing in this manner, from one side to the other can be continued indefinitely. To restore the glider to level flight, push the stick forward, straighten out the rudder and level off."

I was pleased that the student was able to demonstrate this maneuver. After practicing awhile, I requested him to turn downwind for a landing on runway 18.

The next student was Cadet June, one of the best in this group. This would be his last flight before graduation. The TG-2 Schweizer had just started its takeoff roll when a tow plane dropped a triple towrope across our runway dead ahead. June was at the controls in the front seat.

"June," I said, "be sure and jump that rope."

"OK!" he responded. When we got to the rope, June pulled the stick back, but the glider did not have sufficient airspeed to lift off in time to stop us from snagging the line. At the end of the runway, we had attained an altitude of 1,000 feet, with 500 feet of towline caught in our nose skid. We stayed "on tow" until reaching an altitude of 7,000 feet, which gave us some time to figure out a solution. We knew we had to get rid of the rope or use parachutes; any landing attempt would be suicidal. The rope could catch on any solid object, causing the glider to nose dive to the ground.

I said, "June, I'm taking over!"

"OK," he agreed, relieved. "It's all yours."

I put the glider through a whipstall, but to no avail, the rope was still there. I thought, if I had a knife I could cut through the floor and try to unhook the towline. But there was no knife, and we did not have the time; we were in a glide, continuously losing altitude to maintain control.

I leveled off and told June to take over. I told him to fly straight and level, no turns, and hold a constant 60 mph.

"I'm going out on the right wing and see if I can figure out how the rope is caught by looking over the edge. If I fall off, you are to immediately jump. Do not attempt a landing. Is that clear?"

"Yes," June said, concern showing on his face.

"That is an order," I replied.

I opened the hatch, and with my parachute on, I climbed out on the right wing and crawled over to the edge. I cautiously peeked over and saw the rope was caught by a simple loop, which could easily be unhooked if we could get the glider into a vertical position. I started back to the rear seat when an AT-6 came zooming by, the pilot frantically trying to tell us we had a problem. I didn't need this distraction, so I thumbed my nose at him on one of his passes, hoping he would go away. June kept the glider level at 60 mph as requested, a fine job of flying. I made my way back to the shelter of the rear seat, fastened my seat belt, closed the hatch and told June I was taking over. If we were not successful in ridding our glider of the towrope, at 2,000 feet I would order June to jump. As soon as he cleared the glider, I would follow. My mind raced with these thoughts as I pushed the stick forward to reach 100 mph; I then pulled the stick straight back, going into a vertical climb. As our airspeed dropped, I used the stick to keep the glider in its vertical position. As it started to slip back into a "whiplash" maneuver, I pulled the stick all the way back. The glider whipped over into a part vertical, partially inverted nose-down attitude, and I saw the towrope falling free as it accelerated toward the earth. We were free. I returned the controls to June and told him to do whatever he felt like, but bring us back to the base!

❖   ❖   ❖

In our fleet of gliders we had two, three-seater Aeroncas. The factory had installed a third seat in place of the engine; one instructor was supposed to instruct two students on a shared basis during the flight. I did not like this concept; my preference was one instructor and one student in any given aircraft. Besides, the increased weight changed the center of gravity as well as the glide ratio. However, I was elated when the CO informed me that I was to ferry one of the Aeroncas to a new U.S. AAF glider school in Greenville, South Carolina. Another instructor would ferry the second Aeronca to the same destination. Rather than using a double tow, we decided each glider would be towed by its own AT-6 tow plane. We planned to take off the next day at noon on a heading of 165 degrees. We would fly over Charleston, West Virginia, then on to Winston-Salem, North Carolina, passing over both the Appalachian and Blue Ridge Mountains. The last leg would be from Winston-Salem to Greenville. The distance from Columbus to Greenville was 375 miles. At 100 mph, we should arrive at 1600 hours.

The next morning, I picked up my orders at 1000 hours, which were as follows:

"Staff Sergeant Mark B. Bagley is to proceed to Greenville, South Carolina to assist in the transition of Conventional Civilian Flight Instructors to Military Glider Pilot Training Instructors, at the newly formed U.S. AAF Advanced Flying School operated by civilians. Signed by the Commanding Officer, Lockbourne Army Air Force Base, Lockbourne, Ohio."

Both Aeronca TG-5s and their tow planes were ready for takeoff on an apron adjacent to runway 18. After completing a pre-flight inspection of glider and parachute, I boarded the TG-5 and signaled the ground crew that I was ready for takeoff. The glider lifted off at 60 mph, and the tow plane lifted off at 70 mph, retracting his landing gear. We climbed at the rate of 1,000 feet per minute and leveled off at 8,000 feet. As soon as the second tow plane and glider came alongside, the tow planes increased their airspeed to 125 mph, which was OK for the TG-5s. We maintained a heading of 165° for 1½ hours when Charleston, West Virginia came into view.

A cold front was moving in fast, with deteriorating visibility. My tow plane started to climb, while the other tow plane remained at 8,000 feet. My assumption was that the tow plane pilots decided via radio communication to fly at different altitudes, to prevent a possible collision. Soon my tow plane had disappeared from sight into a solid fog bank; it got very dark, and I had difficulty seeing my wing tips. My thoughts went back to the Wolf glider when, under similar conditions, the hatch went flying off. Thank God the Aeronca was better built! My worries switched to thinking that the towline might break. Here we were at 9,000 feet, with no visibility, trying to maintain the proper tow position above the tow plane. I decided that if the towrope broke, I would bail out rather than attempting to walk the glider down over the Appalachians. After an hour or so of this blind flying, I noticed the towrope angle relative to the centerline of the glider had become much wider, which indicated I was too far above the tow plane. It also meant that he may be letting down.

I pushed the stick forward and regained the proper towrope angle. Our altitude was dropping at the rate of 500 feet per minute, with no improvement in visibility. Twelve minutes later, we popped out of the cloud formation at 3,000 feet over Charlotte, North Carolina. We would be in Greenville, South Carolina in one hour. At 1630 we arrived over the Greenville Airport at 1,000 feet. The windsock was indicating an easterly breeze, for our landing on runway 9. The approach was over a dry riverbed, which was fifty feet below the airport. My final approach to runway 9 was too low for the headwind I encountered. I would be lucky to make the runway!

At 200 feet from the end of the runway, I dove down to the bottom of the riverbed to pick up airspeed. The glider went out of sight from those watching near the hangar area; it gave the illusion of "disappearing" into the ravine. Then suddenly, it seemed to rise out of the earth. When I came to a stop at the very end of the runway, they told me it was a spectacular landing. Actually, it was stupid on my part–I acted as if I were flying a sailplane!

I rode in the jeep sent out to tow in the glider. As the jeep approached the hangar, one of the civilian flight instructors said, "Sergeant, that was a wonderful demonstration of precision flying–hope you don't expect us to do that."

"No," I said, "nothing that drastic."

My tow plane pilot refueled and made ready to fly back to Lockbourne that evening. The other tow plane and glider never arrived at Greenville. They must have gone down somewhere in the Appalachian Mountains; I never heard from them again.

❖   ❖   ❖

We scheduled a general meeting of the instructors' group in the hangar at 0900 hours.

The next morning, the chief pilot picked me up at the motel and we drove to the hangar where twelve civilian flight instructors were waiting. After my introduction, I gave the following briefing:

"Gentlemen, I am not here to teach you flying–I am here to help you make the transition to a U.S. AAF Military Glider Training Center. That sounds simple, because it is. You are going to teach yourselves. I'm going to train two of you, the chief pilot and one more. They in turn will teach the rest of you. I'm supposed to give you instructions in single, double and triple tows. But, gentlemen, we only have one, three-place Aeronca, the TG-5. Right now you have several AT-6s, and you will eventually get your glider allotment. The more gliders we have in the air, the more glider pilots we can produce. Tow planes are expected to take off with a glider in tow, climb to 5,000 feet, signal the glider to release, return to the field, drop the towrope, land and be ready for the next tow all in a ten-minute period. To do this, the tow plane must take off at 70 mph and climb at the rate of 1,000 feet per minute."

"Question," said one of the flight instructors. "We can't take off at 70 mph, because the AT-6 stalls out at 90 mph. We'll be killed."

"I'll demonstrate how that's done when your chief pilot and I make our next tow," I replied.

I then explained to them that in the military, it is a court martial offense for the tow plane to cut a glider loose without notification. If necessary, you can bail out, but you cannot cut him loose without his consent. Flap your wings when you want him to release.

Another rule: If the towrope should break at any time on your takeoff run, do not slow down or attempt to abort the takeoff—the glider may end up on your back! Push the throttle all the way forward and move out.

"The TG-5 will be on the runway at 1300 hours," I continued, "with the chief pilot and one other instructor. The tow plane pilot is to take off and climb at 100 mph. That is all, gentlemen."

The chief pilot then dismissed the group. In the meantime, I met with the ground crew and gave them their specific instructions.

The tow plane and glider were ready for takeoff in the warm-up area at the end of the runway. After pre-flighting both aircraft and parachutes, I stationed the chief pilot in the front seat of the Aeronca. The second instructor sat in the center seat, leaving me the rear seat. I signaled the ground crew that we were ready for takeoff, and he in turn signaled the tow plane pilot. I advised the two instructors that I would fly the takeoff and advise them when I wanted them to take over the controls (the Aeronca was the only aircraft equipped with triple controls).

I lifted off at 60 mph and climbed to ten feet above the tow plane. Our airspeed went to 100 mph before the tow plane lifted off. We were climbing at the rate of 500 feet per minute. I explained that our position of ten feet above and on dead center was proper for the single tow. I then demonstrated the proper position for the double and triple tows, as well as all low-tow positions.

"Seat number one, take over and demonstrate the six tow positions that I just demonstrated," I said. The chief pilot did very well in all six positions.

"Seat number two, take over and do the same." He also did very well.

"Seat number three is taking over," I said, then demonstrated how to eliminate slack in the towline and how to keep the line tight to avoid slack from forming.

"Seat number one, take over," I said. The chief pilot again took over and I told him, "Climb up to fifty feet above the tow plane, nose down, and when the tow line becomes slack, release the tow line. The TG-5 flies just like an AT-6 with a dead engine; you're on your own to bring us back to base. Just pretend it's an emergency landing and your engine quit."

The chief made a three-point landing on runway 9 without any difficulty. I then told them that on our next tow (in ten minutes), the instructor in seat number two would transfer to seat one and take charge of instructing and checking out[5] the new instructors in seats 2 and 3. The chief would fly the tow plane, and I would go along as a check pilot. It took the ground crew ten minutes to ready the next glider flight at the end of runway 9. The chief pilot got into the front seat of the AT-6 tow plane, and I buckled up in the rear seat. I told the chief to make his normal takeoff. We got the OK to roll from our line and the chief applied full throttle. At 60 mph, our towed glider was in position, ten feet above our tail, in dead center. We climbed to 2,000 feet, at 500 feet per minute when I said, "Chief, I'll take over."

I told him I was not moving the throttle, but would control our airspeed by elevator control only. I pulled the stick back until the airspeed decreased to 70 mph.

I said, "Notice our airspeed is 70 mph; we are not stalled out and our rate of climb is now 1,000 feet per minute. This proves you can take off at 70 mph with no danger of being killed."

I continued, "It also means you can double the number of glider tows in a given eight-hour period by getting them to 5,000 feet in five minutes instead of ten."

At 5,000 feet the chief signaled the glider to cut loose, after which he dove for the towline drop zone and landed runway 9. He taxied over to the hangar, parked, leaned out the fuel mixture and allowed the 600 horsepower to coast to a stop.

"OK", I said, "that's it. You and your instructors are on your own. I'm going to call Lockbourne and have them send an AT-6 pick up for transportation back to the Lockbourne Army Air Base."

"Sergeant," he said, "there is no need to call them; I'll be glad to fly you back in one of our planes."

"That's fine", I said, "but I have another favor to ask. I noticed you have a gull-wing Stinson in your hangar and wondered if you would check me out. I'd like to fly it for an hour or so, making touch-and-go landings."

I was surprised when he said, "Let's go!"

---

5 The casual term for having one's flying skills approved.

He signed the Stinson out to me and I had a wonderful time flying an hour or so, just having fun. That afternoon, I checked out of the motel and met the chief pilot at about 1400 hours. We boarded the AT-6 and headed for Lockbourne, Ohio. The flight was uneventful and we landed at the base at 1800 hours. We had the plane refueled for the return flight and the chief took off at 1830 hours, turned to a heading of 165° for Greenville. Before disappearing into the twilight sky, he flapped his wings in a sort of farewell salute.

    ❧   ❧   ❧

I was looking forward to seeing Mary after spending several days in Greenville without her. When I came home, she looked beautiful, as she always did. We celebrated my return by going out to dinner in a nearby restaurant.

I arrived at the air base the next morning around 0900 and could hardly believe my eyes. Parked on the apron was the biggest glider I had ever seen! I soon found out its wingspan was actually 83' 8", the length 48' 3" and its high wing was 6' 9" above the ground. Its wing could easily pass over the wing of a DC-3 with eighteen inches of clearance.

The inside was 18' by 6 ½' with full headroom. It had seats along each side for thirteen airborne troops—a seven-seat bench on the starboard side and a bench for six on the port side. The seats were removable and it could accommodate a jeep with machine gun and crew, or an antitank gun and crew, or an automobile. The single glider door was aft, just past the six-seat bench. Passengers would be sitting with their backs against the windows on both sides, so the clearest view would be through the huge glass nose section.

After taking in as much as I could of this immense aircraft, I went over to the operations office and asked, "What's going on?"

I was told that I was one of the eight instructors scheduled to meet with Major Mike Murphy (the head of the Army Air Force Glider Program) the next morning.

The tow plane was warming up on the apron adjacent to the runway, with the glider parked nearby. Major Murphy greeted us as we boarded, and told the first instructor to sit in the co-pilot's seat. He said for the rest of us to pick our own seats and that each of us would get a turn at flying after our release from the tow plane. Murphy stated that this was a CG-4A glider—"C" for cargo, "G" for glider. Our newest glider flying school was in Stuttgart, Arkansas, and consisted of CG-4A gliders exclusively.

The tow plane had completed its warm up and the ground crew had connected the "D" plugs to both the CG-4A and the DC-3. The towline was much heavier, seventy to eighty pounds for its 350-foot length. Its diameter was 3/4" nylon, as contrasted to our lighter lines of only 3/8" diameter hemp. Its tensile strength was over 15,000 pounds instead of a few hundred. Major Murphy picked up his headset and throat mike, and called the tow plane to say he was ready for takeoff. As the tow plane moved out slowly, the slack came out of the nylon rope, which began stretching like a rubber band. The major released the brakes and we started our takeoff roll. We lifted off at 70 mph, climbed ten feet above the tow plane and waited for him to lift off. At 90 mph, the tow plane cleared the runway, climbing at the rate of 800 feet per minute, at an airspeed of 110 mph. We leveled off at 6,000 feet, cruising at 140 mph. Major Murphy advised the crew of the tow plane that he was releasing. He pulled up fifty feet, nosed down and released. He then let each instructor take his turn at flying from the co-pilot's seat.

When my turn came, I was amazed at the visibility in all directions while sitting in the Plexiglas nose section. The glider controls were smooth and friction-free. I slowed to 80 mph, and made several gliding "S" turns before giving up my temporary seat to the next instructor. After the last instructor had his turn, we were down to 1,000 feet. At this point, the major again took over and made a 180° gliding turn to the final approach to runway 18. He applied spoilers all during the 180° turn and released them just prior to touchdown at 60 mph.

The weapons carrier picked us up at the glider and returned us to the operations office. Major Murphy told us that we would be moving to Stuttgart shortly, but that tomorrow *I* would be ferrying the CG-4A to its new home. He selected one of the other instructors to go along as my co-pilot.

In the morning, I met the pilot and co-pilot of the DC-3 tow plane in the operations office. They planned a 0900 takeoff, and estimated we would arrive in Stuttgart at 1400 hrs. We would remain overnight and leave the next morning at 0900 for the return flight to Lockbourne. My co-pilot, Staff Sergeant Younger, came in and I introduced him to the DC-3 pilot and co-pilot.

"We're going over to the hangar to pick up the bird; we'll meet you at the north end of runway 18 for takeoff in ten minutes," said the pilot.

Younger and I picked up our parachutes, caught a jeep ride to the runway, pre-flighted the glider and boarded. The tow plane taxied into its takeoff position on the runway. After buckling my seat belt and putting on the throat mike and headset, I called the tow plane, "CG-4A to DC-3, over."

"Go ahead, CG-4A."

"The ground crew has completed our tow line hookup. We are ready for takeoff, over."

"Follow me!"

The glider lifted off at 60 mph. We climbed to ten feet above the tow plane and leveled off. We used trim tabs to make adjustments and maintain our position, even with hands off the controls. The tow plane leveled off at 5,000 feet with unlimited visibility.

"DC-3 to CG-4A, over."

"CG-4A to DC-3, go ahead."

"DC-3 to CG-4A, this is the pilot. Our navigator has given me a heading of 225° for Stuttgart, Arkansas. We will be flying over Cincinnati, Ohio and Memphis, Tennessee. Our elapsed time is estimated at five hours. The total distance is 675 miles. We estimate our arrival in Stuttgart will be 1400 hours Eastern Time, which is 1300 hours Central Time. We will keep you advised when these cities come into view. Over."

"CG-4A to DC-3; thanks for the report. Instead of flying over the heavily populated areas, I'd appreciate it if you'd fly over the farmlands and open fields . . . circumvent the cities. At 1,000 feet we don't have much time to pick the best forced landing site in the event we lose our towline. Over."

"DC-3 to CG-4A; Roger, Wilco."

At 1000 hours the tow plane advised us that Cincinnati, Ohio was visible off our starboard side. I asked Younger if he would like to take over.

"OK," he said.

"It's all yours. Let me know when you get tired."

I released my seatbelt and took a little walk around the passenger section to stretch. Then I went back and re-buckled myself in. After flying for two hours, Younger decided he'd had enough, at least for a spell. I again took over and estimated we would be over Memphis in an hour and a half.

Younger and I had both been using the rudder to maintain our position relative to the centerline of the DC-3 tow plane. At an airspeed of 140 mph, the rudder was as hard as a rock and required considerable force to operate. I decided to hell with using the rudder; it is really designed for control at much lower airspeeds. I put my feet up on the dash and used only aileron control for holding our current position. It was much faster and a lot less tiring. The next hour and a half went by much more quickly.

The radio came alive once again:

"DC-3 to CG-4A, come in."

"CG-4A to DC-3, go ahead."

"If you look off to your port side, you will see Memphis, Tennessee; we estimate Stuttgart to be thirty minutes flying time."

"CG-4A to DC-3, Roger."

I told Younger, "I know you're anxious to make the landing, so take over for the balance of the flight. I made the takeoff, and it's your turn to make the landing. Good luck."

He was elated. "When you cut loose, I'll handle the radio since it is only connected to the left side controls," I said.

At 1330 hours the tow plane advised that we were over Stuttgart Army Air Base and runway 29 was their active runway. "You may release whenever you're ready," said the tow plane pilot. I relayed this to Younger and told him to release at his discretion. As soon as Younger released, I called the tower.

"Stuttgart tower, this is Army CG-4A in free flight, altitude 5,000 feet, requesting landing instructions."

"Army CG-4A, you are clear to land number one, runway 29. Wind is easterly at 10 mph, altimeter setting 29.92, traffic is right hand, over."

"Roger. We will call on our downwind leg."

Younger made a series of letdown maneuvers and turned onto his downwind leg. I called the tower and reported that we were on our downwind and ready to turn base. The tower acknowledged and confirmed we were still number one landing runway 29. Younger turned base and in a few seconds turned final. We were in perfect alignment at 300 feet over the end of runway 29. It was a perfect three-point landing; smooth, with no bouncing. A weapons carrier came out and towed us into the glider parking area. The flight had been uneventful, and because of that, enjoyable.

The next morning we got on board the DC-3 for our return trip to Lockbourne. The DC-3 crew allowed Younger and me to take turns flying the DC-3 as co-pilots, which to us was thrilling. I had never been in a DC-3 and had only dreamed of flying one!

We landed at the Lockbourne Air Base around noon and reported to the operations office. Major Murphy came in and stated he had received terribly gruesome news about an event in St. Louis, Missouri. He produced a newspaper article that stated the following: "The Robertson Company decided to demonstrate one of its production gliders by presenting a public flight with bands, a huge crowd of civilians, factory workers and many members of the press on hand. The CG-4A was loaded with plant executives and local dignitaries, including the Vice-Mayor. The glider was in free flight over the airport. One of the wing fittings broke, allowing the glider to lose a wing and crash in front of the crowd. No one survived."

Major Murphy made the following announcement: "Flight Instructors Staff Sergeants Bagley, Burrows, Manard and Younger are assigned to the Boeing Aircraft factory in Wichita, Kansas as Army Air Force Acceptance Test Pilots for the CG-4A gliders being produced. Orders will be cut and may be picked up tomorrow morning at 0900 hours, at Headquarters Squadron, Lockbourne Army Air Base."

The four of us met with the major in his office for briefing. He explained that he wanted each production glider to go through a rigorous testing, pulling three to four G's. Load factors of this magnitude are achievable by abruptly pulling out of a high-speed dive, which would test the construction integrity of the CG-4A by imposing a forward or backward whipstall. This maneuver produces excessive load on the tail assembly, as well as high wing load when pulling out of the resulting dive.

"OK, gentlemen, that's it," he said. "Good luck! Pick up your orders tomorrow at 0900 hours at Headquarters Squadron."

That evening, I gave Mary a run-down regarding our relocation to the Boeing plant in Wichita, Kansas. We packed our belongings, loaded the car and settled with our landlord, who lived downstairs.

The next morning, we ate breakfast out and picked up our travel orders, which authorized POC travel to our new destination.

Just prior to leaving, I decided to pick up a few items at the PX. I parked the car and was walking toward the front door when a smartly dressed lieutenant emerged. I rendered a salute and the officer executed the customary return. Just before we passed, he said, "Sergeant, it's Cadet June, your student. I graduated as a 2nd lieutenant! How is it possible that a student can graduate with a higher rank than that of his flight instructor?"

I replied, "Perhaps it was because you received such outstanding grades and demonstrated that you don't panic in emergencies."

I told him about my new assignment to Boeing in Wichita. He wished me luck and we shook hands. I wished him the same and happy landings.

Chapter 5

FLIGHT-TESTING THE CG-4A

Wichita, Kansas

Mary and I arrived in Wichita, Kansas in September of 1943, four days after leaving Ohio. We were authorized to travel via POC, but a speed limit of 35 mph still imposed throughout the U.S. doubled our driving time.

We arrived at the Wichita Airport to discover a group of aircraft factories located on the Southeast side–Boeing, Stearman, Cessna and Beechcraft. Of the four, Boeing had the largest factory, producing six CG-4A gliders daily. The end of runway 27 was closest to the factories. They preferred this runway for takeoffs and runway 9 for landings. The other two runways, 18 and 36, crossed the East-West runway at mid-field. Looking down on the airport from 5,000 feet, the runways formed a perfect "X."

I walked over to the Boeing hangar and asked to see the Army Acceptance Officer (AAO). After the gate guard made a phone call, a lieutenant came out and introduced himself as the AAO. I handed him my orders and told him I would appreciate a couple of days off to locate an apartment before reporting for duty.

"That's fine," he said. "There's so many new factory workers that housing is hard to come by, but good luck!" He told me he'd process my paperwork and have my Boeing pass and flying orders ready when I returned.

Mary and I drove toward town, looking for rental signs. About a mile from the airport, Mary spotted a man putting up a "For Rent" sign. We pulled over and told the man we had just arrived and needed a small apartment. He showed us around; it was a three-room apartment, with a common bath we would share with the tenants next door. We were not too happy with this aspect, but as housing was in such demand, we could live with it. The front door opened onto an enclosed porch with a traditional wood floor, one step above the walkway.

We unloaded the car and set up housekeeping. Mary fixed a wonderful fish dinner, the way only she knew how to do. Afterwards, we took a closer look around the unit and discovered a railroad track in our back yard! Our apartment was fifty feet from a curved section of track that ran right through the yard. That night, around 2300 hours, the pounding vibrations caused by a heavy freight train awakened us. Its headlight, shining through the bedroom window, grew brighter and brighter, directly proportional to the decibels produced by the pistons, drivers and steam from the locomotive. As the train rounded the curve in our yard, the headlight beam moved away from the window and the sound decreased gradually.

The next morning, Mary went into the bathroom and came out in tears.

"What's wrong?" I asked. She led me into the bathroom and pointed to the tub. It had a dirty yellow ring around it and looked very uninviting. I put on my uniform and banged on our neighbor's door. When he opened it, I insisted he look at the bathtub. The previous night, the tub had been sparkling clean. We had not used it; someone from his apartment did and left it like that.

"Charlie," I asked, "was it you?"

"Yeah, bud."

He had taken a morning bath without cleaning up the tub. I told him and his roommate, "The next time I find a dirty bathroom, I'm going to padlock the door until you send someone to clean it!" They both agreed it would not happen again; and it never did.

❖   ❖   ❖

It was time to report to the Boeing plant and start testing the CG-4As. I picked up my Boeing ID and flying orders from the AAO and reported to operations. I ran into Staff Sgt. Younger in the operations office; he and I were scheduled for a test flight at 1400 hours. We picked up our parachutes and headed for the flight line, where a DC-3 and a CG-4A were ready for takeoff. As we entered the glider, Younger said I could pilot and he would co-pilot if I wanted. He had made several test flights, but this was my first.

We began our takeoff run down runway 9. The tow plane made all the communications with the control tower for takeoff clearance and instructions. For obvious reasons, the glider made all communications with the tower for landings.

The takeoff was smooth and easy, which I attributed to the use of trim tab control in place of direct elevator control. The tow plane leveled off at 7,000 feet and I released. I then called the tower, requesting clearance to land on runway 9.

The tower came back, "CG-4A, this is Wichita tower; you are cleared to land number one on runway 9. Over."

I glanced at Younger and told him we would dive to 6,000 feet to build up airspeed, then pull out using full elevator control to produce three to four G's, then climb straight up and let it fall off into a whipstall.

WICHITA, KANSAS
RUNWAY LAYOUT

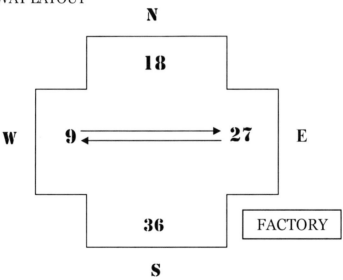

I began doing exactly as I had outlined and was *more than thankful* our wings stayed on during the four G's we pulled as we came out of the dive. We were now climbing vertically and approaching the stall. I asked the adventurous Younger which way he wanted to drop, frontward or backward.

He replied, "Frontward; it's more violent!" As the glider came to a halt in its vertical climb, just before it started its backward slide, I applied full up-elevator, holding the control yoke all the way back. The glider slid backwards and entered a vicious whipstall, causing the nose to drop over 180°, so we were partially inverted. This imposed a greater negative compression force on the wing struts, which were designed for tension, not compression. We were then satisfied with the structural integrity of the CG-4A's wing assembly.

We were at 4,000 feet and no further structural testing was required. We used another 1,000 feet of altitude to adjust the trim tabs for hands-off flight. This also proved completely satisfactory. The glider was acceptable and we landed runway 9 without difficulty.

Younger and I tested half of the Boeing CG-4As produced, and Manard and Burrows tested the other half. Over several months of testing, we experienced no serious structural defects, no wing shedding, parachute bailouts or accidents. Younger and I aborted one of our flights due to excessive vibration. If vibration is allowed to continue, especially at a critical frequency, it could result in a structural failure caused by crystallization.

I vividly remembered that flight. We had been on tow at 2,000 feet and climbing. Younger turned to me and said, "Our empennage wires are missing!" I looked aft and could not see them either. Then I thought back to 1933, when I was learning to fly in a 1928 oXX-5 Challenger biplane. My instructor, Tony Cirello, was telling me to keep an eye on the wing struts, as they had a habit of "disappearing." Tony already knew the rear left wing strut had disappeared; this was his way of bringing it to my attention. It disappeared because of its continuous vibration. If left unchecked, this could lead to "metal fatigue" and structural failures. I remember Tony changing the RPMs from 2400 to 2425, causing the strut to become visible again. "This can happen to flying wires or landing wires," he warned.

I had turned to Younger and told him, "The tail brace wires are there, but are invisible due to the vibration. Let's cut loose and get this thing on the ground before we have to bail out!"

He immediately reached up and hit the towrope release lever. The DC-3 seemed to accelerate as the big cargo glider slowed and the distance between the two increased. Younger was already on the radio to the Wichita tower, requesting immediate clearance to land. He entered the downwind leg and made a 180° left-hand approach to runway 9. We rolled to a stop at the Boeing hangar's main door. We entered the results of our flight in the ship's logbook, as we always

Mark Bagley (far right) and his instructor, Tony Cirello, (3rd from left) pose in front of a Challenger biplane with friends (l to r) "Bananas," Herbert Sharp and Charlie Davenport. Date unknown

did after a test flight. Our report of encountering excessive vibration of the tail bracing cables meant that it must be corrected prior to U.S. AAF acceptance of the glider.

The next day, the same glider was back on the flight line for another go-round. I checked the log, and found that Boeing had readjusted the cable tensions on the empennage assembly. This time, Younger and I found it free of vibration and fully acceptable.

This kind of testing went on until the fall of 1942.

          ❖   ❖   ❖

The Stearman Aircraft factory next to Boeing was turning out primary training airplanes for both Army and Navy flight schools. The only difference between Army and Navy Stearmans was that the Chrom-Moly[6] tubing on the Army's was painted with a red oxide primer, while the Navy specs required bluish zinc chromate[7].

---

[6] An alloy of chromium (a hard metal used for making stainless steel) and molybdenum (a brittle metallic element). When mixed, it is a strong but light steel used in aircraft construction.

[7] Bluish in color, it is "painted" on to protect Navy aircraft from saltwater corrosion. Likewise, red oxide protected Army planes from rust.

The Navy sent in ferry pilots to fly these training planes to various fields. After takeoff, about forty miles out, their engines would stop. Several pilots had to make forced landings. Finally, the factory sent a mechanic to find out what was going wrong. He could find nothing. After restarting the engine, he assumed all was well and went on his way. The Stearmans continued to stall regularly. Some factory personnel decided the Germans had a secret weapon that could short out electrical magneto impulses. I was skeptical and decided to investigate the situation.

All Navy aircraft were painted at the end of the production line, just before leaving the hangar. I climbed up on one that had just come off production and was fully fueled. I had encountered a similar problem when I had refueled the old Challenger, so I thought awhile and then checked the center section where the fuel tank was installed.

Most aircraft engines have fuel pumps that supply pressurized fuel to the carburetor. The Stearman engines did not use fuel pumps, but depended on a gravity fuel-feed system, which meant that its fuel tank must be mounted at a higher level than the carburetor to establish adequate fuel flow.

The fuel tank was installed in the upper wing, about five feet above the carburetor, which produced a static head of 1.60 pounds per square inch (PSI) for adequate gravity fuel feed. For this system to work, the fuel tank must be vented to prevent fuel flow from causing negative pressure. At first glance, this plane seemed to have no gas tank vent. As I searched for it, I discovered the vent was there, but had been taped over with masking tape and painted as the aircraft moved through the paint production line. That's why everything seemed fine when the engine was first started, because gas was flowing from the pull of gravity. But as the plane flew, the closed vent produced a vacuum, stopping the flow of fuel. Once in the air the engines "mysteriously" died out due to fuel starvation.

*   *   *

The Navy sent a group of pilots to pick up the primary trainers for delivery to their Flight Training Center in Pensacola, Florida. This was the first time they had ever seen a CG-4A.

I was sitting on the ramp, almost ready for takeoff. The ground crew was connecting the D plug from the glider to the tow plane. They walked over, curious looks on their faces. One of them opened the rear door and asked if it would be OK to go for a ride. I said, "Sure, hop in!" All five of them piled in and sat on the side benches. I told them that this was not a test flight; there would be no violent maneuvers. I was simply testing the trim tab adjustments for correct range ability, hands-off control and stabilization. The ground crew advised that the tow plane was ready and we had clearance for takeoff.

We started down runway 27. The takeoff was smooth and we climbed to 5,000 feet. I made the trim tab adjustments and accomplished the purpose of my flight. I then radioed the tower for clearance to land. After pulling a couple of wing-overs to impress the Navy guys, I started my downwind turn. On final approach to runway 9, I noticed a B-17 on my starboard side on his approach to runway 36. It looked like we were both number one to land, but on intersecting runways. In other words, we were on a collision course! I radioed the tower; there was no response. I tried several times, but no one acknowledged.

When in flight, gliders have the right-of-way over powered aircraft, military or civilian. But I was not in a position to argue with this guy.

When the B-17 made contact with his runway, I could see the telltale puffs of smoke from his tires. This also confirmed my realization that we would both be at the intersection at the same time! The only advantage I had in a glider was the ability to trade airspeed for altitude, or vice versa. I chose to increase airspeed. The B-17 was about a quarter of the way down the runway, leaving two black lines behind him. He had apparently applied full brakes. I was not yet on the runway, but had excess airspeed. I felt I had enough airspeed to jump over him if it came down to it. The B-17 came to a stop at the very edge of the runway crossing. I had to make absolutely sure my calculations were correct. I pulled the yoke back; the glider responded by crossing the intersection at fifty feet. I then applied spoilers and brakes to slow us down. As we taxied to the ramp, the Navy pilots chatted about the flight, remaining blissfully unaware of our close call.

❖   ❖   ❖

Fall was turning into winter and Boeing was transitioning from making CG-4As to four-engine B-29 bombers. They were to produce only a few dozen more gliders before the changeover. As it happened, they were short one pair of wing struts for their last one. I was assigned to fly a DC-3 to Minneapolis and pick them up. I met with the pilot and we agreed to leave the next day at 0800 hours.

The next morning I arrived at the Boeing ramp with fifteen minutes to spare. The gas truck was just pulling away, after topping off our wing tanks. The Crew Chief was busy removing the control surface locks and landing gear lockdown pins. The pilot was sitting at the navigator's table, reviewing his charts. As soon as the Crew Chief got on board and fastened the doors, we started the engines and taxied to the warm-up area at the end of runway 27. We revved up the engines and checked their operation. We set the fuel mixture controls at full rich for each engine, checked each engine's fuel pump pressure and turned on two emergency electric fuel pumps as an added safety measure. We didn't want an engine failure on takeoff due to lack of fuel. I checked the flying controls, aileron, elevator and rudder to make sure all external locks had been removed. I made sure the engine cowlings were open and set the flaps at 10° for takeoff.

We requested clearance for takeoff and soon the radio crackled, "Army DC-3, cleared for takeoff runway 27. Barometer 29.92, wind northwest at twenty." After the pilot pushed both engine throttles to the firewall, it was my job to hold them in place to prevent changes due to vibration and to free the pilot to make other control adjustments. I noticed that we were drifting toward the right side of the runway. The pilot was applying full left rudder to compensate. We were still pulling toward the edge; the pilot applied full left wheel brake. We had picked up enough speed so that our rudder was active and able to control the drift.

When we had sufficient airspeed to take off, the pilot came back on the yoke abruptly. We sort of "bounced" off the runway into the air. During our climb to 10,000 feet, the airspeed as well as rate of climb were constantly changing. I concluded that this was going to be one hell of a flight. First of all, he failed to pay attention to the wind direction and velocity report from the tower. "Wind northwest at twenty" meant we had a 45° crosswind at 20 mph to runway 27. Crosswind landings or takeoffs always produce a weathervane effect on the aircraft. A crosswind from the right would turn the aircraft to the right. The pilot should have started his takeoff run on the right side of the runway. Secondly, he failed to lock his tail wheel in its center position; it was free to swivel. Third, it is much smoother to take off with one finger on the trim tab control rather than horsing around with the yoke.

We had been flying at 10,000 feet for two hours on a heading of 12°, practically due north from Wichita. The temperature inside was around 65°F and dropping. I was cold; we only had our summer uniforms on and no flying jackets. I asked the pilot to turn on the cabin heat. He replied, "Doesn't work." A cold front had moved in to the Minneapolis area. In a half-hour or so, we spotted the city on the horizon. We let down to 2,000 feet and the pilot called the tower.

"Minneapolis tower, this is Army DC-3 at 2,000 feet south of airport. Request straight-in approach runway 36. Over."

"Cleared for a straight-in approach, runway 36, wind northwest at fifteen, barometer 29.87."

"Roger; four minutes 'til touchdown."

We went through a landing checklist, and made sure we each had a wheel in sight. To my surprise, this pilot was excellent at landings.

We taxied over to the Boeing hangar, shut down the engines and opened the cargo doors to load the CG-4A's wing struts. While they were loading, we went into the factory office, had a hot cup of coffee and tried to get warm. The pilot was anxious to get back to Wichita before dark. Factory workers loaded and tied down the pair of struts. We got back on board the airplane and the Crew Chief closed and locked the huge cargo doors. We started the engines and the pilot contacted the tower.

"Army DC-3, request clearance to active runway warm-up area."

"Clear to taxi to runway 36 warm-up area. Barometer 29.86, wind northwest at twenty. Ceiling is 8,000, visibility ten miles."

We taxied over to the warm-up area and went through our checklist once again. As we taxied onto runway 36, he opened the throttles. This time, however, he was on the right side of the runway because of wind from his left. And again, his tail wheel wasn't locked. It will suffice to say it was a rough takeoff.

At 3,000 feet, we disappeared into the cloudbank. Visibility was zero; we could barely see our wing tips. We climbed to 10,000 feet and headed due south for Wichita. Suddenly, all the instruments went haywire! The airspeed fluctuated between 90 and 225 mph, and the compass was swinging 30°. The artificial horizon and bank-and-turn instruments were unsteady. The pilot was desperately trying to regain control of the plane, but to no avail. I had already been very cold and was now becoming airsick. So, I asked if I could take over the controls for awhile. He replied, "Absolutely!" I could find nothing wrong with the instrumentation. The pilot was causing the problem himself. He had leveled off at 10,000 feet, with all instruments at their correct readings for very smooth air. I picked up a radio range station on frequency 3105 and flew the range stations all the way to Wichita. I asked the pilot if he would like to take over again and make the approach and landing. My attempt at courtesy became amazement as he said, "OK, but I hate airplanes. I'll be glad when the darn war is over and I can go back to my farm." He had made good approaches and excellent landings, but he was not proficient in any of the four fundamentals of flying.

I arrived home utterly bushed. Mary took my temperature and sure enough, I had a fever. Even after a bowl of soup, I was still cold. She decided to call the doctor. After examining me, the doctor announced I had contracted pneumonia. I was to stay at home on bed rest for one week. Mary made sure I had all my prescriptions, hot chicken broth and plenty of water. During my recovery, she taught me how to knit, purl, cast off, pick up, count rows and other knitting functions. By the end of the week, I was working on a cardigan! It was a strangely enjoyable diversion from flying.

I returned to work for more flight-testing of the CG-4As. After one of my morning flights, I saw a full colonel just outside the Boeing office. As I approached, he said, "Sergeant, would you like to go with me to the Quartermaster's in Kansas City to pick up some winter flying jackets?" Recalling my bout of pneumonia, I immediately replied, "Yes, Sir!" He told me we would fly down in a C-45 twin-engine Beechcraft parked on the apron. As we boarded the plane, I noticed it was equipped with nine Norden bombsight stations, used for training bombardiers. The Colonel stated that it was his responsibility to train the new bombardiers assigned to the new B-29 Superfortress produced at the Wichita plant. The Colonel explained that when the crosshairs are adjusted on the target, the bombs were released automatically.

I sat in the co-pilot's seat and we were soon at 5,000 feet heading for Kansas City. I noticed that the starboard engine was about to run out of fuel. We had another full tank, which should have been switched into the starboard engine. Normally, I would have brought this to the pilot's attention, but I wanted to see what his reaction was when the power failure occurred. After all, he must be a damn good pilot to be a full colonel.

In two or three minutes, the engine started a rapid series of backfires. The Colonel was instantly on the alert and started flipping the fuel management switches like crazy! He finally found the right one and the engine roared back to life.

He snarled, "Did you notice that engine was almost out of fuel, Sergeant?"

"Yessir."

"And why did you not call it to my attention?"

"I just wanted to see your reaction," I said. "We were in no danger; at 5,000 feet, you had ample time to get it up and running again." He grunted something and went back to what he was doing. I then asked if I could go back and look at the Norden bombsights.

Looking through the sights made distant targets look closer. I tried lining up the crosshairs, but the system was not operational. I returned to my seat just in time for the Colonel to make a beautiful landing in Kansas City. I commented, "Sir, that was a perfect three-point landing!"

We picked up the jackets and were 5,000 feet up on our way back to Wichita. He asked if I would like to fly the Beechcraft. "Yes, Sir," I replied enthusiastically, and took over for the last fifteen minutes of our flight. I thanked him for my jacket and told him never to leave important details to the co-pilot.

I checked in with the Acceptance Officer, a 1st lieutenant who advised me that I had been promoted from the rank of staff sergeant to flight officer. He told me that I could purchase the uniform, but could not wear it until I was discharged as a staff sergeant and sworn in as a flight officer at some future point. He also advised me that Boeing was closing down their CG-4A production in about two weeks. He told me that I would be getting new orders soon and to continue normal glider testing until then.

When I told Mary of my promotion, she was thrilled and said that we absolutely must buy the best tailor-made uniforms available: Hart, Shafner and Marx, Woolf Brothers or Hickey-Freeman—and nothing less! The next day we went to Woolf Brothers and ordered a complete wardrobe, which we could pick up in one week.

❖   ❖   ❖

It was early November 1942, and everything was changing. Glider production was terminated, I was wearing a new uniform and we were vacating our apartment. I had received my POC travel orders from the Boeing office, so Mary and I packed up our 1939 Plymouth and headed for Stuttgart, Arkansas. We went south to Oklahoma City, then east to Little Rock. From there, Stuttgart was about fifty miles southeast of Little Rock.

We made it in three days and I reported to the U.S. AAF base. My orders stated that I should report to the 313th Troop Carrier Group, but upon my arrival, the CO told me that the 313th had vacated the base several days earlier. He sent me back to Wichita for amended orders!

So, we drove back to Little Rock and spent the night in a first-class hotel for our trouble. The next three days were spent getting back to Wichita. This time, my orders sent me to the Southeast Air Force Training Command, Headquarters Squadron, Stout Field in Indianapolis, Indiana.

I hadn't been paid in a month, and we were running short on cash due to expenses incurred on our useless run to Stuttgart. I didn't have enough money to get us to Indianapolis. I called my Aunt Agnes, in Bedford, Massachusetts and asked her to send $300 via Western Union. I also asked the 1st lieutenant if he knew the location of the nearest government finance office. He gave me an address in Kansas City. The next morning, the Western Union money showed up at our hotel and we headed north for Kansas City, about 150 miles away.

We chose a nice motel near the finance office and Mary rested while I went over there to clear things up. I met with a captain and explained my predicament. He told me that my promotion to flight officer was retroactive and at a higher pay grade. I told him that I would be staying at the motel for the duration of the war, or until all the pay that was due me had come through—including the expense reports I just submitted—because I could not afford to support the U.S. AAF! I gave him the phone number at the motel and told him to contact me when the transaction had been completed.

The next day, a man from the finance office called and asked me to come over. When I arrived, he had it all figured out. He said, "This is complicated, but it is correct. We are going to pay your back pay as a staff sergeant, to the date of your appointment to flight officer. We will pay you as a flight officer up to today's date. We will also reimburse you for your travel expenses to date." He handed me three separate checks and offered to cash them on the spot if I simply endorsed them. I thanked him for all his efforts on my behalf.

Mary and I left Kansas City the next morning on the three-day drive to Indianapolis. The trip was uneventful, but seemed to last forever due to the restricted speed limit and the fact that Mary wanted to get out and stretch at regular intervals. We stopped at picturesque spots, and I snapped several photos.

Upon arriving in Indianapolis, we located a hotel about two miles from Stout Field and checked in. The first thing I did was send a money order to my aunt to repay her for the loan.

After breakfast the next day, I reported to the Southeast Training Command, Headquarters Squadron. I gave my orders to a sergeant in the orderly room, who after reading them said, "I'll see if Major Murphy will see you."

He returned after a few moments and ushered me down the hallway. The major was sitting at his desk. I walked in, saying "Staff Sgt. Bagley reporting, Sir!"

He said, "Forget the salutes," and invited me to sit down. He told me the first thing I had to do in order to accept my new appointment as a flight officer was to pass a physical test.

I returned to the orderly room, where I was officially sworn in as a flight officer.

Mary was delighted that I could now wear my new uniform. We celebrated with champagne before dinner at the hotel, during which I was wearing the uniform, of course!

The next morning, Major Murphy called me on the PA system to report to his office. When I got there, he said, "I'm cutting orders to assign you Burrows, Manard and Younger as check pilots to make sure the glider pilots of the 313th are ready for overseas duty."

He went on to say that he wanted me to evaluate their proficiency. Were they flying correctly and competently? Were they skilled or mediocre pilots? Could they properly demonstrate a forward slip, side slip, turning side slip or a chandelle[8]? Major Murphy's voice snapped me out of my musings. "Pick up your orders at 1600 hours today in the orderly room. Good luck!"

I picked up my orders and met Mary at the front door. We decided to stay one more night and get a fresh start to Laurinburg-Maxton Air Base, my new duty station, in the morning.

That evening, I mapped out our route. I told Mary we would travel south from Indianapolis to Nashville, Tennessee, then east to

---

[8] A chandelle is a unique maneuver efficiently converting airspeed into a 180° turn, with a gain in altitude, requiring no pilot coordination but lots of practice.

Winston-Salem, North Carolina and from there to Laurinburg-Maxton Air Base, which was, strangely enough, in both North and South Carolina. We would be traveling 800 miles. With twenty hours or more driving time, it would take us four or five days.

Although we began early, and nothing eventful happened during our trip, our progress was slowed by the air raid practice drills at several locations along the way.

Just after we crossed the South Carolina line, I spotted a nice looking shopping plaza. I told Mary I wanted to go to the butcher to buy a surprise lunch. She wanted to know what I was getting, but I put what I bought in the trunk to hide it and to keep it cool. After about a half-hour, we came to a lovely wooded area. We could see no houses for miles; it might have been a state park. It was exactly what I was looking for. I pulled well off the highway and retrieved my package from the trunk. I told Mary, "I'm going to fix your lunch, let's find a good spot!" Mary was reluctant to go "off the beaten path," but she followed me. I gathered some kindling from dead branches and built a small fire. I found green tree branches, small in diameter and around eighteen inches long, to use as skewers to cook the meat. I finally gave in and told Mary we were having frankfurters. She agreed it was a treat to be able to enjoy them outdoors. You can't beat the combination of glorious fresh air, sunshine and good food!

I used my jackknife to whittle a point on the skewers and slipped the franks on. I handed one to Mary. I told her that as soon as the fire died down, we could start cooking. I said, "Just pretend you are cooking marshmallows." In a few minutes, the juices bled out and caused the fire to flare up. I told Mary that when they split open, they were ready to eat. "Be careful," I said. "Let it cool down a bit, then slide it off the skewer and take a little bite." Mary loved it; said she never realized that frankfurters could taste so good and could hardly wait for the second one. When we finished, we put the campfire out by saturating the embers with drinking water.

Mary announced it was her turn to drive, and about an hour later we entered Fayetteville, which was only a few miles from Laurinburg-Maxton. I said, "Let's check into a hotel here until we can find an apartment." We drove around and found one that looked promising. At the front desk, we found their rates to be reasonable and decided to check in.

I decided to report to the air base, telling Mary that we would probably have several days to find an apartment. We arrived at the main gate, and the MP directed me to the 313th Troop Carrier Group buildings.

Chapter 6

WELCOME TO THE 49ᵀᴴ

Laurinburg-Maxton Army Base, North Carolina

Mary and I continued our drive along the road until we came to a group of buildings with a sign identifying them as the 313ᵗʰ Troop Carrier Group. Mary decided to read her book in the car, while I went inside to the Orderly Room. I presented my orders to a staff sergeant at the front desk.

"Just a minute," he said, "I want to check your 201 file." He came back and told me that I had been assigned to the 49ᵗʰ Troop Carrier Squadron and should report to them. I asked if he could tell me the status of the three other test pilots, Burrows, Manard and Younger. He went back to the files, then told me they had been assigned to the 29ᵗʰ, 47ᵗʰ and 48ᵗʰ Squadrons, respectively. I thanked him and asked for directions to the 49ᵗʰ·

Again, I left Mary in the car and reported to the sergeant at the front desk. He made a phone call asking if he should bring in Flight Officer Bagley. The answer must have been yes, because he escorted me down the hall to the office of the Squadron Adjutant, Captain Rene Hickman. Upon entering his office, I gave the Captain the customary salute and handed him my orders. After perusing them, he said, "Welcome to the 49ᵗʰ Squadron!" I got his OK to spend the next few days looking for an apartment in Fayetteville and gave him the hotel phone number to contact me if necessary.

Mary was thrilled that we had two or three days to locate an apartment. On the second day, we signed an agreement to rent a three-room furnished apartment and spent the balance of the day shopping for miscellaneous household goods. When we passed a furniture store, Mary wanted to go in–something had caught her eye. It was a Lane cedar chest, which Mary had always wanted, in which to store our wool clothing for protection from silverfish and other pests. We had it delivered the next day.

On the third day, I reported to the 49th Squadron and met with Lieutenant Pettyjohn, the Glider Operations Officer. He wanted to know if I had been checked out on gliders at this field. Although the answer was rather obvious, I simply told him, "No."

"You better go down to the line and get checked out, "he said.

I said, "OK," but I didn't go. Instead, I went to the Officers' Club. There I ran into a man who introduced himself as Lieutenant Brist. Brist was filling out an application for Officer-in-Grade training for the cadet wing at Kelley Field, Texas. I asked him where I could get one. He told me they were available at Squadron Operations, but he offered me an extra one he had.

"Where do I file the completed application?" I asked. Brist told me to turn it in to Squadron Ops for approval. He said if my application was approved, the CO would be flying everyone accepted for the training down to Kelley Field. I thanked him and turned in my request that afternoon.

The following day, Mary said she would like to drive me back and forth to the base so she could have the use of the car to run some errands. After she dropped me off, I decided to visit Squadron Engineering. I walked out to the flight line and over to the hangar. An officer sat at his desk and a staff sergeant and a corporal were making changes to their aircraft status boards.

I introduced myself to the lieutenant. "I'm Bob Piser, the 49th Squadron Engineering Officer," he replied. He told me that as Engineering Officer he was responsible for the aircraft and engine maintenance of twenty-five, twin-engine, airline-type DC-3s called "Dakotas" and for the twenty-five crew chiefs assigned to each plane.

Lt. Piser happened to mention that he and his wife had found a rental unit in Fayetteville. "That's wonderful," I said. "Maybe we can share transportation back and forth to the base." I gave him our address and he said it was just down the street from them. When he learned that Mary dropped me off that morning, Bob offered me a ride home. By the time we arrived at my apartment, we had worked out an arrangement to use Bob's car to go back and forth to the base every day; I would pay him for the gas. This would free up my car for Mary and Bob's wife, Evelyn.

For a week or so, I had made regular visits to the 49th Squadron's Orderly Room to look at orders posted on the bulletin board that confirmed my assignment as a check pilot. Going through the proper channels took forever and I was becoming annoyed at the delay. Before anything was posted, I ran into Captain Hickman, who informed me that the CO was flying Lt. Brist and me to Kelley Field to continue the application process for the Officer-in-Grade training. We were scheduled to leave the following day at 0900 hours.

The next morning Bob dropped me off and upon entering the Orderly Room, I saw Lt. Brist and another pilot looking over aeronautical charts, preparing for our flight. Someone yelled, "Atten--TION!" and the CO entered the room. He immediately replied, "As you were," and proceeded to introduce the pilot I did not know as Lt. Tom Crause, his co-pilot. He then picked up his briefcase full of charts and said, "Let's go! I have a driver and command car waiting to drive us to the plane."

The Crew Chief was waiting for us and advised the CO that the aircraft was ready for flight; all external locks had been removed, fuel tanks were full and engine oil levels were safe. However, being an experienced airline pilot with hundreds of hours of flying time, the CO always did his own pre-flight inspection.

The CO finished his inspection and we boarded the plane. He then warmed up the engines, checked the magnetos, RPMs, mixture controls, oil and fuel pressure and instrumentation. After advising the tower that we were ready for takeoff on runway 18, the tower came back with immediate clearance. The CO opened the throttles and you could hear the snarl of the engines as we accelerated down the runway. Halfway down, he executed a smooth liftoff at 90 mph. I felt additional acceleration, followed by a couple of thumps as our landing gear retracted. We were climbing at 1,000 feet per minute. Tom was milking up the flaps, which means he was bringing the flaps up a few degrees at a time, to prevent drastic changes to the plane's attitude. We leveled off at 3,000 feet and 185 mph.

I went back to a window seat overlooking the starboard wing. As I looked out the window, I could not believe my eyes. The gas tank cover was missing and a three-inch diameter gasoline stream was dousing the side of our fuselage. I ran to the cockpit and informed the CO. He rushed to the window, took a quick look and ran back to his seat, picking up the mike and calling, "Mayday, Mayday, come in!"

When the tower responded, he said, "This is Army DC-3 returning to base. We have fuel spewing from our wing tank and spraying all over our starboard aft fuselage. Have emergency equipment on

by." He requested clearance for a straight-in approach to
ay 36 and advised that we would touch down in ten minutes.

ne tower came back, "You are clear for a straight in approach to
vay 36; emergency equipment will be standing by. We are
ling all traffic until after your arrival."

The CO acknowledged with a single word, "Roger."

He then announced that he wanted everyone on board to put on
eir parachutes. If the plane caught fire, we were all to bail out if we
ere above 1,000 feet. He told us, "Don't jump below the 1,000 foot
vel; without a static line to open your chute, you haven't got a
nance."

He then turned to Tom with the following instructions: "We are
going to make a wheel landing." In other words, we were flying in and
touching down at 90 mph, then reducing power and braking. "Do not
use flaps or the usual fuel mixture," he added. The customary rich
fuel would build a fireball between the engine nacelle and wing flaps.
I had noticed how black with soot this area was on DC-3s. It was
caused by burning fuel—which would be fatal in this case.

We let down to 2,000 on our final approach to runway 36. I went
back to my window seat to take another look; the fuel was still
gushing out of the wing tank. I kept smelling for gasoline, but could
not detect even the slightest odor. That's one good thing, I thought. If
I had smelled even a trace of gas, I would have jumped out the door
instantly. The smell of gasoline within the fuselage would signify an
explosive environment, which even the smallest spark could
detonate. The spark might come from an electric switch turning on or
off, such as a microphone switch, or a landing gear switch.

The CO announced over the PA system that we were just below
1,000 feet, on our final leg, for touchdown in one minute. I noticed
that Lt. Brist was getting out of his parachute; my guess was that now
we were too low anyway and he did not want to be hampered by a
clumsy parachute. I figured that was a pretty good idea and followed
suit.

Again I checked the wing tank's gas flow, no change. We were very
low now. The end of runway 36 was passing under our wings and I
barely felt the main wheels make contact. But a puff of black smoke
passed under the starboard wing and the wheels went from 0 mph to
90 mph in a fraction of a second. The engine's RPMs reduced to a
minimum and brakes were applied as we began our deceleration. As
our speed reduced, I noticed that the fuel flowing out of our wing

tank did also. I thought to myself that this was a good example of what we learned in training: *flow is equal to the square root of the differential pressure.* When the tail came down, and we had a three-point landing, further braking made the flow stop altogether.

As we turned off the runway onto a taxiway, the CO shut down the starboard engine and we taxied to our apron. The Crew Chief scrambled to locate a new gas tank cover before having our plane washed down.

We were all relieved when that ordeal was behind us. The four of us on that flight and the Crew Chief agreed that our CO must have experienced that exact situation before, perhaps during his hundreds of flying hours as a pilot for American Airlines.

The gas truck came over and pumped in 150 gallons of fuel. This time the Crew Chief made damn sure the tank cover was fastened down properly. The CO again boarded the plane and announced that we would be about an hour behind schedule for our arrival at Kelley Field. He picked up the mike, and thanked the tower for their help during the crisis. Then we turned onto runway 18; he opened the throttles and we lifted off. I wanted to be sure that we were not spilling fuel again, so I looked out the same window and saw there were no problems.

Lt. Brist was sound asleep on the port side seats. We had been flying for about an hour, when the CO came aft to stretch his legs a little. He sat down next to me and we chatted. He didn't seem to want to talk about his flying experience, but was interested in mine. I gave him the rundown of my experiences to date. He asked how I liked gliders. I told him the same thing I told the officer in Biloxi when asked if I wanted to join the glider program: "If the Army wants me to fly baby carriages, I'm willing—as long as they have wings!" I then said I liked gliders; they were easy to fly and safer than powered planes. But I also told him I thought the glider program was a waste of time. For one thing, there were not many missions suitable for glider use. While gliders did have their advantages, such as landing in short distances and the ability to fly in heavy equipment, it was much more efficient to use paratroops. That usually made it counterproductive to use gliders; after all, a DC-3 couldn't be used as a troop carrier plane if it was towing a glider.

We talked for over an hour. It began to get dark and we could see lights far below. The CO looked out the window and said, "Tom's right on course—there's San Antonio. But what's he doing at 10,000 feet? We're going to need oxygen if we get any higher."

We entered the cockpit and found Tom fast asleep with his hat over his eyes. We shook him, then asked where we were.

"Gee, Major, I don't know . . . the last time I looked over, you were sitting there!" he said. The CO sat down in the pilot's seat and let down to 5,000 feet. He told Tom and me that before leaving the cockpit, he had set the trim tabs for level flight. Just walking aft by twenty feet caused the tail to drop and the plane to climb. After an hour or so, it had reached 10,000 feet.

Soon he picked up the mike. "This is Army DC-3 twenty miles east at 5,000, requesting landing instructions for Kelley Field. Come in, Kelley."

"Kelley Field to Army DC-3 twenty miles out; runway 7 is our active, using left hand pattern. Call on downwind."

"Army DC-3. Roger."

Ten minutes later, he picked up the mike again. "Army DC-3, turning downwind runway 7. Request clearance to land."

"Army DC-3, this is Kelley tower. Wind velocity ten easterly, barometric pressure 29.92 inches. We have you on final; you are cleared number 2 to land."

Tom and the CO went through the regular landing checklist and made a perfect three-point landing. We taxied to the visitors' apron area and shut down both engines.

The CO arranged for a command car to take us to a local hotel. That evening, he treated us to dinner, during which he told us that a command car would pick us up at 0830 hours the next morning and drive us to the base administration office, where we would continue to process for OIG training.

I got up early the next morning, had breakfast and went down to the lobby to find the CO, Tom and Lt. Brist already waiting. At 0900 hours the CO, Lt. Brist and I entered the administration building. There was an officer sitting at the cadet information desk. The CO walked up to the lieutenant at the desk and requested to see the officer in charge of In-Grade training. He came back with a captain, who introduced himself and asked how he could help us. The CO explained the reason for our visit and presented him our applications.

The captain said, "Let me review these; it will take a few minutes, but if they are in order, I'll start processing them immediately." He then went back to his office, but he returned in about fifteen minutes and said, "Both applications look good; I'll start processing them right away." He explained that it might take thirty to sixty days for the approval process, as they had a large backlog.

We thanked him and headed back to the plane. Tom and the Crew Chief had everything ship-shape and ready to go. Soon we were on our way back to Laurinburg-Maxton. Five hours later, we landed. I thanked my CO and got a ride home to Fayetteville with Bob.

Mary was happy to see me and fixed a wonderful dinner. I didn't tell her about our wing tank episode, as I knew it would cause her needless worry.

The next morning, I accidentally ran into Lt. Pettyjohn, who again asked if I had been checked out for flying at this field. Of course, I said, "No."

We headed for the flight line in his jeep. Gliders were taking off and landing every ten minutes. He contacted the glider operations crew on his walkie-talkie, telling them I required a check-out flight for the field and that he would appreciate it if it could be handled right away.

Glider Operations came back and said they had a glider ready for takeoff on runway 18. Pettyjohn responded, "Be there in less than one minute!"

He dropped me off at the edge of the runway. The glider was already hooked up to the tow plane. The tow plane's engines were idling and everything looked ready to go. I walked over to the glider, climbed in and sat in the pilot's seat. As I fastened my seat belt, I noticed the check pilot sitting in the co-pilot's seat was extremely short in stature. He wasted no time reiterating that he was to give me a flight check, so that I would be able to fly at this field.

"That's my understanding also," I replied.

He said, "Check all your controls—aileron, rudder and elevators— to be sure there are no external locks in place. Fly about ten feet above the tow plane. Be sure when you release from the tow plane that you dive, to pick up slack in the line before cutting off. OK, Let's go."

By this time, I was damned fed up with this crap. I had been sent here to check up on these guys and report on their flying proficiency; instead the less proficient were doing the checking! I decided I was going to do the exact opposite of what he told me. No more of this bullshit. The first thing I wanted to show him was a "slingshot" takeoff, and after that, other maneuvers which had yet to be named.

I signaled the ground crew that we were ready for takeoff. Each of the tow plane's engines emitted huge puffs of smoke as they revved up to their full 2,460 horsepower. I applied full brakes and both of the glider's wheels locked.

The check pilot screamed, "Release the brakes!"

"Hell no," I answered, "I'm going to demonstrate a slingshot takeoff. Hang on!"

The tow plane was accelerating fast and the 300-foot nylon towrope stretched to 400 feet. The ¾" diameter rope was now about ½" in diameter. The tensile strength imposed on the towline was approaching 3,000 pounds. The check pilot was having a fit and started cursing. The tires let out a long screech and we went airborne at 60 mph, still accelerating. I maintained level flight until the tow plane was twenty feet above the glider.

The check pilot was going nuts again. "You're supposed to be ten feet above the tow plane, not twenty feet below! Use your rudder to keep it lined up," he yelled. So, I took my feet off the rudder and placed them on the edge of the instrument panel.

"I never use the rudder on tow, it's too tiresome and a waste of time," I said. I climbed to a position ten feet above the tow plane. The check pilot seemed more relaxed and stopped yelling.

I observed a tag number, which indicated Boeing Aircraft in Wichita, Kansas had manufactured this glider. No doubt one of us four test pilots assigned to Boeing had originally flown it, so I knew it had been vigorously tested and proven reliable.

We were at 3,000 feet and I hit the towline release lever. The check pilot almost had a stroke. "I didn't tell you to release!" he said, his voice high-pitched.

"Hang on! I'm demonstrating a whipstall," I replied. Do you want to fall backwards or forwards?"

"Are you crazy?" he asked.

"'Must be," I answered, and we went over on our back. As I finished the whipstall, I advised that my next maneuver would be the "chandelle." Shaken, the check pilot told me to turn back at once, or we would never make the runway. I made a 180° turn and headed back to the field.

"We aren't going to land on the runway," I told the check pilot, who now seemed resigned to the fact that we were going to do whatever I decided.

"We will land on the grass just this side of the runway." I nosed the glider down. Our airspeed of 150 mph was just right. I then told him that we would touch down on the grass at 150, then pull up into a loop with 1.5 positive G's at the top. "Our recovery speed will be about 90 mph at approximately 150 feet altitude. I will then make a three-point landing on the grass."

The maneuver went just as I planned. As the glider rolled to a stop, I undid my seatbelt, got up and opened the door. Before stepping out, I turned toward the check pilot, who was still looking very disgruntled, and said, "Will you kindly inform Lt. Pettyjohn that I have been properly checked out for flying at this field?" Then I went home for the day.

The next morning, Bob dropped me off at the Orderly Room as usual. The first thing I was told was that Lt. Pettyjohn was looking for me. I went to his office, expecting him to raise hell about my flight, but that was not so. He had my new assignment. I was to report to the flight line and start checking out pilots of the 49th Squadron, which was in accordance with Major Murphy's original orders. I told him that I knew what was required of me. I said it would probably take about two weeks to complete this assignment, as there were 49 glider pilots to check out. I told him I would keep a flight report on each pilot and give him my recommendations in a report after completing the testing. He agreed, and I set off for the flight line.

The first glider was ready; the pilot I was to check out was already buckled in his seat. I only had to take a quick look before thinking to myself, "Oh God, it can't be true." It was the same short guy who gave me *my* check flight the day before!

I went over to the co-pilot's seat and buckled myself in. Then I said to him, "Don't worry; it's alright. Remember everything you told me?" He nodded in affirmation. I said, "Well, you were right. Everything you told me yesterday, I want you to do today."

"OK," he replied and signaled the ground crew that we were ready for takeoff.

The engine on the tow plane came to life with a roar and we accelerated down the runway. The glider lifted off first, leveling off at ten feet above the tow plane.

We were at the end of runway 18, at about 500 feet, when our towline broke. We were in free flight. I told the pilot to drop the 300-foot line, make a chandelle and land downwind on the grass alongside runway 18. He followed the instructions exactly; I couldn't have done it better myself. We were just touching down on the grass and I asked him to get on the brakes, as our ground speed was too fast. He said, "I can't use the brakes. I can't reach them . . . I'm too short!"

Well, the co-pilot had no brakes but an otherwise full set of controls. I told him that I was taking over and he agreed. The question I was now asking myself was, "How do you slow down a glider landing downwind, at a ground speed of 90 mph?"

Using the nose skids to brake is risky; the tail wind could flip us over on our back. The only solution I could think of was to fishtail, using the rudder to make a series of S-turns to generate additional drag. We were running out of grass in a hurry. Then I had an idea. I told the pilot, "Hurry, we don't have much time! Take off your seat-pack parachute and place it behind your back. Then see if you can reach the brakes!" He tried it, then replied, "Yes, I can!" I told him to take over control and get on both brakes! The glider came to a stop about 500 feet from the end of the grassy area.

✻   ✻   ✻

One day I was told to report to Lt. Pettyjohn. I immediately went to his office. "There has been a change in your assignment," he said. "The head of the U.S. AAF, General Hap Arnold, is planning to attend flight demonstrations here at Laurinburg-Maxton, probably around the end of February. The demonstrations will include short-field glider landings, as well as larger field landings like landing infantry, anti-tank guns and vehicles. DC-3s will demonstrate paratroop drops from 400 feet and glider snatch tows. After the demonstrations, General Arnold can make up his own mind as to whether or not the 313th Troop Carrier Group, and the four squadrons, the 29th, 37th, 38th and 49th, are ready for overseas assignment."

Upon hearing this, I reminded him that as we agreed, the results of each check ride would not be entered into any individual's 201 file unless my assignment had been completed. I told him that otherwise, I would destroy the individual reports I had generated. I let him know that after completing thirty percent of the testing, the results were as follows: ten percent of the glider pilots should be washed out; twenty percent were marginal, twenty percent average and fifty percent excellent. Then I said, "Operations may think they have a logical solution to these test results—make pilots out of the fifty percent that are excellent and co-pilots out of all the rest. But that would not be the best thing to do. What if glider pilots were ever asked to fly into combat with only one pilot? For what its worth, that's my report."

I contacted Captain Hickman and mentioned to him that I hadn't been issued leave in over a year of service. I wanted to visit my parents in East Foxboro, Massachusetts, and Mary wanted to visit her brother George, in nearby Foxboro. He told me that my leave orders would be ready in three days.

I rushed home to tell Mary about my leave. She was excited and purchased roundtrip Pullman tickets between Fayetteville and Mansfield, Massachusetts.

At 1000 hours, after I picked up my leave papers, we boarded the train. We had previously called our families to let them know we were coming for a visit. My brother John said he would meet us in Mansfield. During our train ride, we enjoyed lunch and dinner served in the first class dining car of the "Merchants Limited," one of the most exclusive passenger trains operated by the New Haven Railroad between Boston and New York City.

We traveled north along the Eastern seaboard, through places like Washington, D.C.; Baltimore, Maryland; New York City (and its Grand Central Station); New London, Connecticut; Providence, Rhode Island; and finally, Mansfield, Massachusetts. Mansfield was a flag stop; passengers could detrain, but no one was allowed to board.

We got off the train and sure enough my brother John was waiting for us. As soon as he spotted us, he rushed over to Mary and said, "Haven't seen either of you since you became husband and wife. Congratulations and welcome home!"

My parents' farmhouse was over 100 years old and located on five acres alongside the railroad tracks. As kids, we watched trains like the Merchants Limited go by, and wondered if we would ever get to ride one of them.

When John turned the car into our driveway, the house looked the same, except for about three feet of snow. My mom and dad were happy to see us. They had prepared a sumptuous roast beef dinner, with my mother's specialty, Yorkshire pudding.

Mary called her brother, who lived about five miles away. He was thrilled that we had arrived and wanted us to come over immediately. I had met him about six years earlier, when I started working at the Foxboro Instrument Company. He was the head of the electronic instrumentation department. Little did I know I would one day fall in love with his sister, who I met when she came in to apply for a job.

Mary and Mark, in East Foxboro, circa 1943

When we arrived, Polly, George's wife, opened the door with a warm smile and a welcome greeting. She served us lobster, which we thoroughly enjoyed.

The next day, George and I toured the Foxboro Company. I couldn't believe it; all the young men were missing. They had all gone off to the war. I even tried to get in touch with my former boss, Al Herschel, only to find that he was serving as a commander in the Navy. I also saw that all their regular production instrumentation was transformed into the production of Norden bombsights and other military devices. Everything seems to go in cycles, I thought.

The following day, we had to draw our visit with George and Polly to a close. I had promised my Aunt Agnes, who lived in Bedford, Mass., that we would stop by for a two-day visit. Mary and Aunt Agnes were "old friends"; I had introduced them about two years earlier, before we were married, and they hit it off immediately. Aunt Agnes had prepared a marvelous steak dinner with all the trimmings; and for dessert, we had her special plum pudding with hard sauce.

After we arrived and settled in, Aunt Agnes informed us that Bedford had a new airport, called "Hanscom Field." It was designed to take some of the air traffic away from Boston, especially if it was closed due to heavy fog.

She asked me if I remembered my first airplane ride. Of course I did, I told her.

It was Memorial Day in 1926 and we were watching a parade. I saw an airplane overhead and when my aunt asked me what I would like to do that day, I said I would like to go for an airplane ride. Soon Aunt Agnes, my brother John and I were heading to the East Boston Airport (now called Logan). We boarded a trolley car near the house, bound for Lexington. We then transferred to another trolley car, which took us to Harvard Square. We then took a subway train to Park Street Station in Boston, then a trolley car, which took us to East Boston, through the Harbor Tunnel. We got off at the end of that line, and took a taxi to the airport.

Somehow, Aunt Agnes was able to find an old biplane with a WWI engine and a pilot who would take John and me for a ride.

As I neared the airplane, I noticed it was shaking as though it were alive. The propeller and engine were making a lot of noise and blowing a lot of air. I decided I was not going. Aunt Agnes replied, "Young man, you *are* going! You and John get into the front seat right this moment. I've had enough of your tricks, so get in!" I had never seen her so upset—so I got in first.

The pilot reached in and fastened our seatbelts very tightly. I couldn't even move. We were not sitting on a cushion of any kind, nor could we see anything but the inside of the cockpit. We took off with lots of wind and noise and bumps. And suddenly, we were airborne.

Then it became peaceful; however, all we could see was the underside of the top wing and a little sky. Finally, our ride was over. The plane came to a stop and the pilot released our seatbelts. After we got out, I told John not to tell Aunt Agnes that we couldn't see anything. After all that trouble, she would be very unhappy if she knew. When Aunt Agnes asked John how he liked it, he said, "It was fine." She then asked me, and I said, "Aunt Agnes, it was wonderful!"

My aunt was a great influence on my interest in aviation. When I was eight years old, she took me to an old barnstorming field, where WWI pilots used to fly their OX-5 Jennies, give rides and do wing-walking and other stunts. I asked her, "Which way do they come in? She answered, "Always heading into the wind." Sometimes they had to sideslip over the high trees, because the field was very small.

In 1927 my Uncle James, Aunt Annie, Aunt Agnes and I sat in the kitchen, looking at the clock and listening to the radio. It was 9:00 p.m. and Charles Lindbergh, who was flying across the Atlantic, was now halfway between Paris and New York. We were awaiting news of his landing and all praying for a safe trip. Everyone was thrilled and relieved when we heard that he had arrived safely. Not long afterward, Aunt Agnes sent me a "Lucky Lindy" helmet.

The first airplane I ever purchased was a 1937 Taylor Cub with a forty horsepower, four-cylinder engine. I'll always remember the number—NC17231. In place of a tailskid, it had a steerable tail wheel. The main gear did not have any brakes.

I remembered landing in a cow field on my uncle's farm. The pasture was 800 feet long by 600 feet wide. There was a five-foot fence all around. I landed into the wind, side slipping to miss the fence around my 800-foot landing zone. I wanted to show Aunt Agnes my plane and let her see it up close.

She asked me to take her for a ride. "OK," I said, but told her I would have to fly over to Burlington and pick her up there. The wind had changed 90° and I had to use a short-field take off. It would have been unsafe to attempt it with her aboard.

The pasture's gate was at the center of the 600-foot side. I opened it up and planned to put the fuselage through the gate if I did not lift off by the time I got there. Beyond it was another hay field that I could use to continue accelerating for take-off.

As I was taxiing into position for take-off, I glanced down and saw that my right wheel was about to drop into a hole. Sure enough, the wheel went down into the hole and a fence post came right through the fabric-covered wing. Brakes could have prevented such a mishap.

Now, repairs to my plane were necessary. But how? My aunt knew exactly where to go to get the materials required. We got beeswax thread, linen fabric rated at 100 pounds per linear inch, pinking shears, glue, brushes and acetone thinner. I completed the repairs in about three hours.

Ready to attempt take-off again, I moved the plane by hand into its short field position, opposite the open gate. I warmed up the engine and opened the throttle. When I was about 300 feet from the open gate, my speed indicator showed 50 mph. All of a sudden, a boy on his bicycle appeared at the gate. He stood stock still for a moment, as he realized an airplane was rushing towards him. I have never seen a kid drop a bicycle and run off so fast in my life. I, on the other hand, lifted off and passed through the gate with no difficulties. I then picked up my Aunt Agnes in Burlington and gave her her first airplane ride.

❖   ❖   ❖

Mary and I had many other things to talk about during our brief visit with Aunt Agnes, but all too soon it was time to leave. We thanked her again for all her support and told her we would write often.

We spent the next night with my parents and the following day our vacation was over. We said our good-byes and John took us to the Mansfield station. After breakfast the following morning, we arrived back at Fayetteville.

When I reported to the squadron, I was advised that General Hap Arnold would be visiting our base sometime that week. I knew that meant we would be putting on our various flight demonstrations, but I wasn't particularly interested. If they wanted me to fly, they would have to ask. "Let them come to me" was my motto!

I went outside and walked along the perimeter road, adjacent to one of our airfields. I knew the field measured 800-feet long by 800-feet wide. A cargo glider was attempting to make a short-field landing. The approach to this field was over a stone wall; the other three sides were lined with tall trees. The glider was making a straight-in approach and I could see he was too low and slow to clear the stone wall. He hit the wall, broke off both wheels and damaged a wing strut.

The ground crew cleared away the damaged glider quickly, so a second glider could make the same attempt. By the time he reached the stone wall, he also did not have sufficient altitude to clear it. He landed in a crosswind along the outside of the wall, but this time there was no damage.

Captain Jackson, the 313th's Group Glider Operations Officer, walked up to me and said, "Bagley, show them how to do this."

I thought to myself, why the hell are they always asking me to do these crazy things? I don't have any more of a chance than the last two!

Arriving over the field at 1,000 feet, I decided to use a 360° overhead approach. I used this type of approach to practice forced landings as a civilian. In this maneuver, altitude is directly proportional to the number of degrees turned. For example, after completing 90° of turn, my altitude would be 750 feet; at 180° of turn, I would be at 500 feet; and at 270°, I would be at 250 feet. In reality, the 360° overhead approach is a continuous, controlled side slip.

At 250 feet, it was time to forget reading instruments, and pay attention to what was happening outside the aircraft. I was about 200 feet above the stone wall, flying parallel to it. I applied full spoilers, which dropped the glider to 100 feet above it; then I made a side-slipping left turn into the field. The glider made a slow three-point landing. I applied brakes and the glider came to rest at mid-field.

It had actually been a nerve-wracking experience for me, because of the four other glider pilots who came along to observe and learn what to do—or what not to do!

Later that afternoon, I was again told to report to the flight line. Operations had scheduled me for a flight at 1500 hours. There was a string of a dozen or so gliders and tow planes lined up on the end of runway 18. My glider was number three in the lineup.

When I opened the glider door, I was very surprised to see a jeep with a .50-caliber machine gun mounted on it, the driver and a 2nd lieutenant infantry officer already inside. They were from the 82nd Airborne out of Fort Bragg, North Carolina. We made our takeoff run, and after liftoff, I leveled off at fifty feet above the tow plane.

Sitting in the co-pilot's seat, the lieutenant turned to me and said, "This is our orientation flight; I would appreciate it if you'd make it short."

In that instant, we parted company with our towline. We were in free flight fifty feet above the runway and close to the end. I said to the lieutenant, "Your wish just came true; this is going to be damn short!" I immediately released the towline, as it was now dragging on the ground. It could snag a tree and pull us into a nose-down crash. I converted our excess airspeed into additional altitude by using the chandelle, in a 180° right-hand turn. I planned to land downwind, alongside our takeoff runway.

I told him not to be alarmed; everything was OK, but as a safety precaution, I was unlocking the glider's nose section. I said the nose would open about 15° and that he would be able to see the ground through the gap in the flooring. I did this to prevent the jeep we had on board from crushing us, in the event that we hit a solid object during landing. The jeep was connected to a lever and pulley system, designed to open the nose section to its full 90° whenever the jeep was moved forward. The jeep would pass under the pilot and co-pilot, but only if the pilot remembered to unlock the nose.

That evening, Mary and I had dinner at the Fayetteville Hotel. A 2nd lieutenant and his wife came over to our table and he asked if I was the pilot who made the forced landing. "That's correct," I said. He then told his wife, "This is the pilot I was telling you about."

We invited them to join us, but they had already finished their meal. As soon as they walked away, Mary wanted to know why I did not tell her about the forced landing. Because I did not want her to worry about me, I simply told her that I forgot.

✢   ✢   ✢

The day finally arrived for General Hap Arnold to review our flight operations. There was a field on the base measuring 1,200 feet by 1,500 feet. We were to land twenty CG-4A gliders in this field, as part of our demonstration. I was assigned to glider number twenty. Naturally, the last one in. As usual, I thought, I was getting the short end of the stick.

Twenty gliders took off in sequence and leveled off at 1,000 feet in a trail formation. I watched as the number one glider touched down near the end of the field and smashed his wing into a telephone pole. Then gliders were landing all over the place. By the time I started my landing pattern, the field was invisible due to all the dust stirred up by gliders using nose skids and brakes to slow down. Even the gliders themselves were not visible, except for their tripod struts mounted on the right side, at the top of their nose sections.

All I could do was land in an area where there were no struts visible. As my wheels touched down, and we were slowing, the plywood floor beneath my seat was suddenly replaced by a tree trunk. They had recently removed some trees from this area, but neglected to remove the stumps.

My next assignment was to demonstrate the "snatch tow" of a CG-4A. For this maneuver, a clear area a minimum of 500 feet is required. The towline is draped in a loop over two poles in front of the glider, ten feet apart. The tow plane is equipped with a twenty-foot-long pick-up pole attached to its tail section, with a large hook at the end. The tow plane also has a hydraulic winch, with 15,000 feet of stainless steel cable. The pilot of the tow plane comes in low, at 150 mph, and "snatches" the glider's towline with the pick-up hook.

When the hook picks up the towline, it sounds like a .50-caliber gunshot. The steel cable starts spewing from the winch at 150 feet per minute. Once the winch comes up to speed, an automatic rapid deceleration brake is applied. In the event that the tensile load exceeds 10,000 pounds, the glider's towline will release. Several 35-mm Army cameras were set up to film the snatch tows[9].

---

[9] This footage was also used in the 1945 movie *Objective Burma*, starring Errol Flynn, George Tobias and Henry Hull.

I boarded the glider. My check of all controls and functions indicated that I was ready to go. I held the control column all the way back, so I could become airborne as quickly as possible. I was trying to sit there in silence; the seconds seemed like hours.

The DC-3 came from behind at 150 mph and twenty feet from the ground. With a tremendous roar, it briefly came into view, but failed to connect with the hookup. On the second attempt, I heard the hum of its twin engines turn into a roar. The tail of the plane flashed into view as it passed overheard and a loud explosion sounded as the tow plane's hook made contact with my towline. The glider accelerated rapidly, from 0 to 140 mph in a few seconds. Our takeoff run was less than 300 feet and in less than a minute, I was at an altitude of 3,000 feet. The tow plane was at 2,000 feet and two miles ahead. He winched us in to our customary 350-foot towline length.

The tow plane returned us to the base and I cut off, landing in the grass alongside the runway. Several additional tow flights were made.

General Arnold must have been very impressed with our demonstrations. Soon after his visit, orders came through stating that all officers living off base were to be assigned to BOQs (Bachelor Officer's Quarters). Wives were to be sent home; the Laurinburg-Maxton Army Air Base was under alert.

That evening, I broke the news to Mary. She took it very hard at first, but we knew that eventually it would come to this. The next day, we packed all Mary's things into her new cedar chest and shipped it to her home in Hollywood. We moved out of our apartment, sold our car and purchased a ticket on the Merchants Limited for her.

She decided to stay with my parents in East Foxboro. Summer was around the corner and this would be a vacation of sorts. The hardest thing I ever had to do was say goodbye and watch her board the train. Downhearted, I waited until it left the station.

I reported to Captain Hickman and told him I needed to be assigned a BOQ. He said there was a vacancy in Building 10 and a sergeant escorted me to my new quarters.

Building 10 consisted of eight rooms; I wondered which one I was going to get. I saw a cat wandering down the long hallway and the Sergeant informed me that it was mine. I also found out that each room in the barracks housed two to four officers, instead of the customary one.

That evening, I had a difficult time getting to sleep. Many guys were in the same situation as I was, and thinking about it gave me a lump in my throat every time. Finally, I was sound asleep, when a couple of slaphappy drunks came in, singing and shouting all the way. Apparently, they'd been assigned to the room opposite mine. After several minutes of hell raising, they decided to take showers. Then they left the room, wearing nothing but their shorts and towels.

When they were out of sight, I entered their room. The walls had yet to be painted and a five-gallon can of paint was sitting on the floor. A newspaper lay on the table. I grabbed it and laid the opened sheets alongside each bunk. Then I put some paint on the newspapers, right where they would step to get into bed. I proceeded to rip open their pillows and put the feathers into each bed, between the sheets. Last but not least, I walked down to the fuse box, unscrewed several fuses and threw them away.

Then I went back to my cot and pretended I was asleep. Soon the drunken "twins" made their way back to their room, still shouting and clowning around. They couldn't figure out why the paper was sticking to their feet! Coughing and sputtering, they tried to get away from the feathers, which were flying everywhere.

They both came out into the hallway, demanding to know who did it. Someone got the lights on again and the two of them came over to my bunk, asking if I was the culprit. One of them thought that I was the one responsible, but the other one said, "Oh no, Bagley would never do anything like this!" I was still pretending to be asleep.

Then they went into the next room, where four other glider pilots were sleeping and accused them. This started a huge ruckus. I, of course knew the two intoxicated fools were Crause and Brist.

Lt. Brist got pushed through a piece of drywall separating a couple of rooms and someone started a water fight using the barracks fire hose. Flight Officer "Doc" Ott was asleep in the room next to Brist and Crause. After the rumpus died down, he came up to me and accused me of soaking his new coveralls. I asked, "How much did you pay for them?" He answered, "Three dollars." I gave him the three dollars; it was well worth it.

The next morning, I stayed in bed until everyone left, except Lt. Brist. When he finally got up and dressed and we were about to leave the barracks, I saw Colonel Roberts, our group CO, coming towards our room. I thought he was coming over to investigate the damage. He was just outside the door, and I said, "Hey, here comes the Colonel . . ." In a loud voice, Lt. Brist replied, "Aww, piss on the Colonel!"

The Colonel came in, went over to Lt. Brist and said, "Lieutenant, I want you to write a 300-word essay on just why you would piss on a colonel. Have it on my desk at 1700 hours today." Before he walked away, he advised us to be prepared to move out at a moment's notice.

A few days later, the train that was to start us on our journey to a top-secret overseas destination pulled into the base railroad station. In less than one hour, 200 glider pilots and ground personnel assigned to the 313th were aboard. As we chugged away, I noticed that the marquee outside the base theatre had a large electric sign out front displaying the name of the feature movie playing, *Casablanca*.

Late the following day, we pulled into another railroad station in New Jersey, Camp Kilmer. This was our port of embarkation. They told us we would be there no longer than three days, no passes would be issued and when the base went to full alert, all telephone service would be cut off.

Max Becker, another glider pilot assigned to the 49th, came to me and said, "My wife and I live close by in Hempstead, Long Island. I'm going home for a visit. If the camp goes to full alert, call me. Here's my phone number." I agreed.

Twelve hours later, the camp went to full alert. Before I could call Becker, telephones were disconnected and military police were guarding the perimeter. I decided to go see Captain Warner, the acting adjutant during our relocation. I told him about Flight Officer Becker and said I wanted his permission to leave camp, call Becker and return. I told him that I did not want to be considered AWOL or a deserter if the MPs picked me up.

The Captain refused to give me his permission. He told me that if I were arrested, he would deny any knowledge of our conversation.

But I decided to go it on my own. Very surreptitiously, I ducked out the back gate. Under cover of the afternoon shadows, I managed to get to a phone and get a hold of Becker.

With no thanks to Captain Warner, I snuck back on base and put that little adventure behind me.

I found it entirely unbelievable that on that same evening (after Becker returned from his "visit"), Captain Warner presented him with a shiny new pair of gold lieutenant's bars. He had been promoted to a commissioned officer! When some other non-commissioned officers and PFCs who had left camp returned, they were arrested and court-martial charges were filed against them.

The next morning, we boarded a train for the waterfront, where we transferred to a ferryboat. An hour later, we off-loaded at the Port of New York, where our steamship was berthed. It was a long walk along the pier from our ferry to the steamer, where troops were in various stages of loading. As I approached the ship, I caught the name on the fantail: the SS *America*. I couldn't believe I was traveling on board this ship! Mary's Aunt Marjorie, now Countess Marjorie de Bouthillier, had married Count Guy de Bouthillier, the *America's* architect.

I stepped off the gangway into a beautiful recreation room. The stairways at each end were so elegant and I soon discovered that the entire ship's design was exquisite.

I was escorted to my quarters, which consisted of a suite of three rooms and a large bath, called the "Warrick Suite." For Mary and me, it would have been heavenly; but having to share it with four other guys made it lose a lot of its appeal.

Several hours later, we set sail for our unknown destination. As the steamer left the dock, I stood outside looking aft. New York City grew smaller in the distance.

I went into the dining room, where a card game was just getting under way. I was invited to join in a game of contract bridge. We were just passing the Statue of Liberty, and I wondered how long it would be before I would see it again.

The SS *America* was carrying over 5,000 troops on her solo Atlantic crossing. She was fast enough to outrun German submarines, with a top speed of 27-29 knots. In order to confuse the enemy, we changed course every six minutes. The windows were boarded up, portholes blocked and no lights were visible from the outside.

After four days, we were out of range for our anti-submarine observation planes. On the eleventh day, we were advised that a German wolfpack of submarines lay just ahead. We were diverted to the Azores, a group of islands 300 miles west of Spain.

I contacted the Chief Engineer of the ship and asked if I could see the engine room. When he asked why, I explained that prior to joining the Army, I was employed by the Foxboro Instrument Company as an instructor. I had trained Navy personnel in the very same instrumentation used on board this vessel. Upon hearing that, he said he would be delighted.

I saw that most of the instrumentation was from the Foxboro Company. I noticed a flashing red light had come on in the alarm annunciator panel, indicating a high water level in the boiler steam drum. The Control Panel Operator acknowledged the alarm and the light went steady. I mentioned to him that he could prevent this warning light by making a simple adjustment to the drum level controller. He said, "But I do; I change the controller set point all the time."

I told him that this was a temporary adjustment, and if he changed the proportional band, it would be more permanent. He then asked if I could explain to him how the three-element drum level system worked. "Sure," I said.

I spent the balance of the day in the engine room, answering questions on instrumentation and controls. The Operator asked if I would come back the next day, as he had some more questions. I promised I would.

I was awakened the next morning by the cry of, "Land ho!" I dressed quickly and went out on deck. In the distance, I saw a beautiful white city rising out of the ocean. It got bigger and bigger as we approached. An hour later, we entered the harbor. I was sorry I would not get back to the engine room as promised, but we had reached our covert destination: Casablanca.

Chapter 7

PLAY IT AGAIN, SAM

Oujda, near Casablanca, French North Africa

Although billeted in Army tents with wood flooring, after two weeks in Casablanca I had still not acclimated to the fine, red baking-powder sand that seemed to permeate everything. We were told that our CG-4As were being removed from their shipping containers for final assembly and would be air-worthy in a few days. Each glider had been shipped in a separate container measuring 10' x 10' x 20'.

At that point, some gliders were already assembled and available, but our group's were not. Although I was eager to fly again after so much traveling, I forced myself to remain patient. It was understandable that they were behind schedule. The 313th consisted of 100 gliders and 200 pilots, which made up the battalion. Each of the four squadrons (the 29th, 37th, 38th and 49th) had fifty pilots and twenty-five gliders, which represented a full complement in accordance with the squadron Table of Organization.

Each squadron had an adjunct of twenty-five C-47s and fifty C-47 pilots, all attached to the 313th Troop Carrier Group. These tow planes were flown from our previous air base, Laurinburg-Maxton, and re-established at Oujda, in French North Africa.

As they were assembled, gliders slowly started to line each side of the runway at Casablanca. They were fully loaded with supplies and their towropes had been attached. Finally, I was told that a complement of five C-47s was en route for glider pick-up. We pilots were issued parachutes, and proceeded with our routine inspections. The tow planes finally arrived, and were refueled and loaded with supplies.

When it came time for my takeoff, a tow plane taxied into the hook up position at the end of the 350-foot nylon towrope. The ground crew inserted the D-plug into the mating connection on the tail of the C-47. I picked up the radio mike. "Tow plane on runway, come in." There was no response. I repeated the message, and this time a voice came back loud and clear.

"That you, Bagley?" I immediately recognized who was speaking. It was Tom Crause. Tom was a good friend of mine; he was courageous, considerate and a good pilot—but sometimes a bit too carefree.

When the headset crackled again, I could tell Tom had opened the mike before he spoke, as the radio picked up the deep rumble of the C-47's twin engines. His voice message came through above the din.

"I'm going to run up these engines again and check the RPM differential between mags; they're running a little rough."

"Roger," I replied.

"The engines check out OK. You ready for takeoff back there?"

"Roger . . . roll it!" I responded.

"Let me know when you cut loose; I want *you* to break loose first, otherwise you'll put me back on the runway."

Tom started forward, the slack came out of the towline and we started accelerating. About halfway down the runway, the airspeed indicator reached 80 mph. I eased back on the control column, and released the towrope. I advised Tom that I was airborne and going to level off at ten feet above him. The C-47 made a smooth takeoff. I retracted the landing gear, and as we approached 120 mph, started milking up the 20° of flaps. We climbed to 6,000 feet on an easterly heading. The Mediterranean sky was beautiful, with smooth air and a temperature of around 70° Fahrenheit at our cruising elevation. I picked up the mike.

"CG-4A to C-47, come in."

"Go ahead. Over."

"Would you mind telling me where the hell we're going?"

"Oujda."

"Well if you have a moment, how about letting me in on this!"

"Got plenty of time. My co-pilot's flying and I'm looking out the window."

He then proceeded to tell me that Oujda was located about 200 or so miles east of Casablanca. "It's in the goddamn desert," he said, about five miles west of the better-known Arab town of Karawan. The Arabs' religion claims one trip to Mecca, or two trips to Karawan, is necessary during one's lifetime. In the old days, it was a French Foreign Legion outpost. The buildings were made of granite and marble and there were no bathrooms, at least not as we knew them. He said there were no toilets to sit down on, "You just stand or squat over a drain in the center of the room."

No running water, either, he said. "We bring bottled water for drinking and cooking." Well water was pumped into a stone sluiceway, which they used for washing clothes. The clearest water was near the beginning of the stream intake, and those farther downstream got the dirtiest water from upstream washings. "It's lousy."

He continued, "The food isn't that great either. We eat out of our mess kits, which is OK, but we have to run to a screen room before the flies completely cover our food. Even in the screen room, we still have to slap away the persistent ones that sneak in whenever the doors open."

The airstrip was now about six miles ahead, he told me, and that I could see Karawan just beyond it. "Land runway 18 and clear it. After you cut free, I'll drop the rope and follow your landing. Good luck!"

"Thanks, Tom! Cutting free. Over and out."

After parking the glider, I found a stretcher and fell asleep in a niche in the ancient French Foreign Legion billeting quarters.

None of the bare rooms had doors, only archways. As I was walking down the hall, I heard a click-click-click sound emanating from one of the marble-lined rooms. When I peered into where the sound was coming from, I found it to be from a small hammer and chisel held by one of our glider pilots, Ed Landell. Ed was probably the oldest glider pilot in the 49th, with many years of flying experience. He was working very diligently at removing the firing cap from a French 75-mm brass shell. I could see he had already removed the lead projectile and gunpowder. Oh, well, I thought . . . he must know what he's doing. Then the firing cap exploded! He was lucky that the powder had been removed; otherwise, it would have been over for him. The only damage he suffered was burns to both hands. Our Flight Surgeon had Ed back to flying in two weeks. Later, Ed claimed to be making a pair of brass flower vases from the shells, to take home as souvenirs.

❖   ❖   ❖

After a week of settling in, I went down to the flight line to see what was going on. Several mechanics and a flight officer were attempting, unsuccessfully, to calibrate an aileron bell crank assembly for a glider's right wing. I checked the logbook and discovered that *none* of several technical orders (TOs) issued from Washington, D.C. had ever been completed. In other words, the gliders at Oujda were not considered airworthy by those in Washington, and should be grounded until such time as these mechanical issues were resolved.

The next thing I did was to inform the CO, a major, that I would not fly any glider that was grounded by Washington. It is a pilot's right to refuse to fly any aircraft that has outstanding TOs. I then told him that I would be happy to make sure that all gliders were in compliance with the TOs. He told me to go see the flight officer in charge of engineering and tell him about my offer; I said, "Yessir!" and left.

But I did not go back to the flight line. Instead I went to my sack. I wrote some letters, played cards, took it easy. About a week went by, and I accidentally ran into that major. He asked, "Have you been down to the flight line?"

"No, Sir."

"Well, why not?"

I told him it was because the line mechanics cannot have two bosses.

"If there is an issue that the existing flight officer and I do not agree upon, then what?"

"Then you both come to me and I'll decide."

"Yes, Sir!"

But I again went to my sack. About another week slipped by before I ran into him again. For the second time he asked, "Have you been down to the flight line?"

"No, Sir! I'm not in a position to assign myself to those responsibilities."

"OK, Bagley, you win . . . you're the new Engineering Officer for the 49th Squadron gliders."

I couldn't help but smile as I said, "Major, would you please cut such an order and put it on the bulletin board, with a copy in my 201 file?"

He didn't say yes or no, only, "You are dismissed!"

I decided that if the order was issued, I would respond at that time.

❖   ❖   ❖

The 313th Troop Carrier Group managed to fly 100 C-47s across the Atlantic Ocean without attracting the enemy's attention. No medals of any kind were issued for such bravery. In regards to that remarkable voyage, I asked Tom, "Did anything special happen on the way?"

"Yeah," he said, "there was one thing. When we first entered the southwestern Sahara Desert, our twenty formations of five planes each must have been very impressive—especially to the lone ME-109 that kept buzzing us, and looking us over. We were letting down for refueling at a base in that area, and to our amazement, the ME-109 circled until all the C-47s had landed. He then turned downwind, came in for a landing and taxied over to where the lead plane, Col. Roberts, had parked. He cut his engine, got out and surrendered."

Tom continued to say that when the pilot was asked why he wanted to surrender, he said he knew he was outnumbered and could have been shot down at any moment. He wondered why we chose not to. Colonel Roberts accepted his surrender and informed him that we were all transports. With the exception of our .45s, we had no weapons.

As Tom finished the story, we started our let down to Casablanca. The next day, we loaded the plane with all kinds of things: hospital supplies, food, canned goods including cases of fruit cocktail and crates of all sizes and weights. The difficulty with loading is to ensure that the center of gravity (CG) remains in the same general area. To do so, we used a slide rule to track the weight and location of each item. When we completed our loading, we found the CG to be acceptable.

Tom warmed up the engines. We were conducting our pre-flight inspection when we noticed a truck approaching us at a high rate of speed. It pulled alongside, and the driver announced there was a forgotten item, which turned out to be a damned heavy electric generator, complete with gas engine and automatic controls.

The only place available to lay it down was at the entrance to the single door. We retrieved our slip sticks and determined that its location and weight did not create a dangerous CG change. To make sure we were not tail-heavy, I reverted to a previously known test

91

procedure I used as a rough rule-of-thumb. I climbed out of the plane and walked around to the tail; I placed my back underneath the horizontal stabilizer and lifted it approximately four inches, which in my experience meant that everything was hunky-dory.

After loading the generator, we tested it and once again the C-47 did not show tail-heavy. We again warmed up and were cleared for takeoff. During our takeoff run, I noticed that Tom lifted the tail early. I asked him how it felt; he said it seemed fine.

We were scheduled to fly to deliver some of our cargo to Tunisia, but it was getting dark as we approached Oujda; Tom decided to lay over and continue on in the morning.

We ate dinner and were sitting around the sorry excuse for an officer's club, when Major Stovall, the Squadron Operations Officer, came by. He told us that another crew was going to complete the flight to Tunis. The newly assigned crew needed their four hours flying time this month to receive flight pay, and several more pilots were in the same situation.

The next morning, the new crew took off at 0700, under foggy conditions. The ceiling was at 500 feet, with one-mile visibility and negligible wind. Their takeoff looked normal, but minutes later we received a radioed message, "We are turning back!"

That was the one and only message we ever received. The plane was found approximately three miles east of Oujda, but there was nothing left of it. About 200 feet west of the crash site, there was a fifty-foot long slash in the sand. They had radioed that they were turning back, but they must have been too low. Their wing tip slashed into the sand, throwing the plane into a violent cartwheel.

In this accident, we lost a pilot, co-pilot, navigation officer and a crew chief. For the 49th Squadron, these were the first casualties, but by no means the last. We would lose eighty percent of our C-47 pilots in the next three years of the war.

The Major called Tom and I into his office and asked if there was anything unusual about the flight that may have contributed to the crash. Tom told him that we observed nothing out of the ordinary. The hydraulic systems, fuel management manifold, gauges, engine instrumentation, radio, emergency fuel pumps, landing gear, trim tabs, elevator, rudder, aileron controls and autopilot were all functioning normally. We also checked the plane's logbook for any discrepancies and for red diagonal markings or Xs, which indicated a problem. We could find no such entries. The Major then asked if we had any theories as to what caused the crash. Tom offered nothing specific, but my theory was that low-lying fog made it impossible for the pilots to distinguish between the sand and sky. Very few pilots had ever encountered such dangerous meteorological conditions.

Because the conditions in the French Foreign Legion housing were so primitive, we were billeted in Army tents. Wood flooring did not exist there, only desert sand. We placed each leg of our cots in a can of kerosene, to keep the scorpions from climbing into bed with us. Tom and I were assigned to the same tent, and we set our sights on installing a floor.

Tom picked up a jeep from the motor pool. We had seen a sort of junkyard nearby, with all kinds of older Italian and German military equipment. We figured the proprietor was in collaboration with the enemy, and were wary of him. However, he had actual *tile* and an Italian motorcycle that Tom was itching to ride. Tom advised the owner that we would send over a weapons carrier the next day to pick up the tile and that he would like to borrow the motorcycle. He told him that both of these items would be returned whenever we left the area.

A few days after we completed laying our new tile flooring, I ran into the Major coming out of the mess hall. I saluted as he came towards me, and after rendering a salute, he stopped short.

"Bagley! That junkyard owner paid me a visit yesterday. He wants his tile and motorcycle back. I would appreciate it if you would return his things."

"Yes, Sir. I'll look into it," I replied.

He then asked how things were going on the glider flight line. I told him very well; we had reinstalled a stubborn bell crank assembly, made control cable adjustments and put all the gliders back on line.

Later, I told Tom what he said about the return of the junkyard goods. It must have pissed him off, because he replied angrily, "Just leave it to me. I'll take care of it." Exactly what happened I don't know . . . but we kept both the tile and the motorcycle.

❖ ❖ ❖

Our Squadron Officer, Flight Officer Hamilton, had posted orders for Flight Officer Benbow and Flight Officer Durkee to bring a fully loaded CG-4A from Casablanca to Oujda. As Squadron Glider Engineering Officer, I made it a point to advise them of their

93

engineering responsibilities and how to deal with the sub-depot. I told them to do the following: Check the logbook for any grounding TOs that have not been completed and make sure you get a glider first aid kit, external spoilers, a tie-down kit, external control locks and a walkie-talkie.

I advised them that they would not be able to do a complete inspection, because in order to do so, the glider would have to be unloaded. And, last but not least, I told them, "If you don't get all the items I mentioned, don't sign the acceptance paperwork. Ask for another glider. Be sure to get the serial number of any glider you turn down. And one more thing, because this glider hasn't flown since it got here, request a towing altitude of at least 6,000 feet. Good luck!"

Benbow and Durkee were gone for two days. They finally returned, without the glider. "What happened?" I asked. "Did you refuse to accept the glider, and if so, do you have the serial number?"

"No," Benbow replied, "nothing like that."

Being from the Mt. Shasta, California area, they both did a lot of pre-war flying in mountainous terrain. They never hurried to get anything done, but they were very precise and possessed good flying skills.

Benbow explained that they were on tow at 6,500 feet, about an hour out of Casablanca, when the glider suddenly started a series of outside loops. The towline wrapped around one of the wings and soon snapped. Meanwhile, the glider was still making outside loops. For unknown reasons, the controls were unresponsive. Cargo was moving in all directions. They decided to bail out, but could not get to the door because the cargo had shifted.

Benbow said he kicked out the window on his side of the glider and jumped out.

Then Durkee spoke up. He said that after Benbow got out, he started to make his way towards the same window, but the cargo shifted again and was partially blocking his way. He struggled to make it to the open window, and jumped. He said he pulled the ripcord and prayed his chute would open. It did, and as Durkee looked down, he said he was shocked. He couldn't see Benbow anywhere!

Durkee said he yelled out, "Benbow! Where are you?"

Then he had a sickening thought. His chute must not have opened! Poor Benbow . . . I guess he didn't make it. He jumped first and now I don't see him. But he continued to call, "Benbow, where are you?"

Then a loud voice that seemed to come from the heavens answered, "Durkee, I'm right here!"

"Where are you? I can't see you!"

"I'm about ready to walk all over your parachute!"

When they were back on solid ground, Durkee asked Benbow in amazement, "How did you get up there? You jumped first, so you should have been below me. I thought you were dead!"

At the close of their hair-raising story, I said, "Well boys, I'm glad you were wearing your parachutes; otherwise, you wouldn't have had a chance. And remember what it says in the Bible: 'The first shall be last . . . and the last shall be first!'"

❖   ❖   ❖

One morning I was on the flight line, waiting for a tow plane to show up so I could take one of our gliders on a test flight. A jeep driven by a colonel came into view. Sitting in the passenger seat was a staff sergeant; they both wore the 82nd Airborne insignia. As they pulled alongside me, I saluted the colonel and he acknowledged.

"Are you Flight Officer Mark Bagley?"

"Yes, Sir."

"I am the CO of a regiment of 82nd Airborne paratroopers. I have someone here who would like to see you."

The Staff Sergeant jumped out of the jeep and ran around to my side. To my surprise, it was none other than Dominic La Fratti. He gave me a big hug and we shook hands. Before the war, Dominic and I kept our airplanes in the same hangar at the Plainville Airport in Massachusetts. We both lived a short distance away, Dominic in Attleboro and I in East Foxboro.

Dominic's plane was a Nicholas Beasley, a high-wing monoplane with an open cockpit. It had a seven-cylinder, air-cooled radial engine. At that time, I had a high-wing monoplane with a closed cockpit—a 1937 Taylor Cub.

I asked Dominic how he knew my rank and our group's location. He said he called my mom, who told him I was a flight officer, stationed at Laurinburg-Maxton. She said I was assigned to the 82nd Airborne, working on their first glider maneuvers. He said the rest was easy; the Colonel had tracked down my unit's location.

The Colonel interrupted our conversation and asked if it was possible to have a glider ride.

"No problem," I said, "we already have spare parachutes inside."

They both checked the packing dates on their parachutes and put them on. I offered the Colonel the co-pilot's seat. The tow plane arrived and the ground crew connected our towline and interphone cables.

As we started to move, I explained to the Colonel that we would lift off at 60 mph, climb to our cruising altitude, then level off at our standard position ten feet above the tow plane. I told him and Dominic that on tow our airspeed would be 140 mph, but in free flight, it would vary from 60-80 mph, at the pilot's discretion.

When I cut off at 6,000 feet, I turned the controls over to the Colonel and suggested that he fly from our current altitude down to 4,000 feet. Then Dominic could fly the glider from 4,000 to 2,000 feet. I would regain the controls for final approach and landing. Out of respect for his rank, I made sure the Colonel was OK with our plan.

When the Colonel was flying, he did not do very well. His turns were not smooth, our airspeed fluctuated almost constantly and his left wing was too low.

At 4,000 feet I took over, while Dominic and the Colonel switched seats. When I turned the controls over to Dominic, his flying was perfect. All his turns were controlled and precise. So when we got to 2,000 feet, I said, "Dominic, it's all yours. Go ahead and land runway 18. Just make a rectangular approach, using a left-hand pattern." He did exactly as I instructed, and at 200 turned final at the beginning of the runway. I told him his airspeed was perfect and after touchdown, to turn off at the first taxi strip. We rolled to a stop, got out and soon the ground crew picked us up in a jeep to take us on the short ride to the flight line.

Both the Colonel and Dominic thanked me for the glider ride. I shook hands with the Colonel and thanked him for bringing my good friend over for a visit. As they left, I shook hands with Dominic and told him how good it was to see him again. I wished him the best and said I definitely hoped to catch up with him in Massachusetts after the war.

I stopped by the squadron engineering office to see my friend Bob Piser, the power plane Engineering Officer. When I arrived, the first words out of his mouth were, "The CO wants to see you."

I wondered what I had done now. The CO was not busy, so I went into his office and gave him a salute.

"You wanted to see me, Sir?"

He stood up, held out his right hand and said, "Congratulations, Bagley! You have been approved for Officer-In-Grade flight training at the Air Force Advanced Flying School at Kelley Field, in Texas. Lt. Brist has also been approved and has already left."

I asked, "What is my next step?"

"Take these approval papers to General Eisenhower's office in Tunis. We dispatch courier planes daily to Tunis and Casablanca."

He handed me the documents, and I thanked him, saying, "I'll be on that plane tomorrow!"

The next day I arrived at General Eisenhower's headquarters in Tunis, and found it impossible to see him. After waiting several hours, I was able to see his adjutant. I told him the reason for my visit and handed him my paperwork for Kelley Field. He simply said, "I'll handle it. You are dismissed." I saluted and left.

I stayed overnight at a very nice hotel. While I was there, I wanted to see Carthage. To me, it seemed filled with ancient mysteries. Its narrow-gauge railroad would take you anywhere you want within the city. I saw a well-preserved Roman coliseum, which I remembered reading about in high school history books. I didn't have time then, but someday after the war, I wanted to come back and see more.

I returned to Oujda the next morning and reported to the CO. I told him what happened and that the adjutant said he would handle my orders. The CO replied, "All hell has been breaking loose ever since you left. Headquarters is pissed off; so is Troop Carrier Command, Wing and Group. Colonel Roberts (the Group CO) called me and laid it on me for allowing you to go directly to Eisenhower. They are all upset because I did not go through the proper channels. And if that wasn't enough, Eisenhower was furious. No one is to be reassigned from this command, especially to receive additional training. We have a long war ahead. . . ."

"Well, Major," I said, "I only have one question. How did Lt. Brist make it out?" He had no answer.

"Anyway, thanks for helping me get approval for the training. . . ."

The order sending me to Kelley Field never materialized.

❖   ❖   ❖

Major Andrews walked into the squadron Engineering Office and asked me if I would like to be Glider Engineering Officer for the 313th Troop Carrier Group. I told him I would love to.

"Congratulations," he said. He told me that I had been pre-approved, and that he'd talked to Captain Myers, another 313th Engineering Officer. I was to share his office. Colonel Roberts had agreed as well.

The next day, my CO issued an official order and posted it on the bulletin board. It read, "In addition to his other duties, Flight Officer Mark B. Bagley is appointed Glider Engineering Officer for the 313th Troop Carrier Group."

There was a second order posted. "Flight Officer Ben Grogman and Flight Officer Mark Bagley are ordered to ferry a CG-4A from Casablanca to Oujda ASAP. Grogman will pilot, and Bagley will co-pilot. The tow plane will be piloted by Lt. Tom Crause."

I immediately checked with Tom. He said, "How about we leave at 0800 tomorrow?" I told him that would be OK with me.

We took off at 0800 sharp. Besides Tom, Grogman and me, there were two other crewmembers aboard: Lt. Burton, the DC-3 co-pilot, and our crew chief.

At around 0945 we landed in Casablanca. Tom taxied over to the glider flight line, where we hooked up the one we were supposed to fly back to Oujda. The glider's 350-foot towline was neatly coiled and wrapped with wire, fresh from shipping. Each coil weighed ninety-five pounds. Because it was also loaded down with cargo, I checked the glider's weight and balance, and found it to be OK.

The question was, should we leave for Oujda now, or wait and leave after lunch? We all voted to have lunch there in Casablanca, because of the good food. The food at Oujda was referred to by many as "shit on a shingle."

We left Casablanca around 1300 hours, under sunny skies and moderate winds. I was wearing the wool vest that Mary knitted for me after I came down with pneumonia in Wichita. We were about two hours out (280 miles), at 7,000 feet. The ambient temperature inside the glider started to climb, and I took off my jacket and Mary's sweater vest. A short while later, it became cool again. I put my jacket back on, but folded Mary's precious gift over the back of my seat. Apparently, we had passed from a warm area to a cold front.

I was sitting peacefully in my seat, when I decided to check in on Tom via the interphone. As I was reaching over to pick up the microphone, I noticed something unusual. A coil of the heavy nylon towrope was lifting off the cargo area floor. It continued to float upward. It was about four and a half feet off the floor and headed directly towards me. I put out my arm and pushed it away.

It went plunging downward and crashed through the cargo floor. At the same time, the tow plane dropped 200 feet in a fraction of a second, causing the glider to accelerate and drop downward in turn. That sent several of the coils smashing through the glider's roof.

I could see an astonished face looking out at our glider breaking up; it was the DC-3's Crew Chief looking aft through the astronavigation dome on the back of the tow plane's fuselage.

The series of violent updrafts and downdrafts continued. We lost all our cargo, either up through the hole in the roof, or down through the hole in the floor. I saw my sweater sucked out through one of the holes in the floor. Amazingly, it came back in through a different hole! I unhooked my seatbelt, and tried to make my way over to where the sweater had caught. But as we hit another downdraft, I was bounced off the glider's ceiling. I finally reached my precious sweater and decided it was time to bail out.

I made my way over to the door and called out to Ben Grogman, "Let's get the hell outta here!" Ben answered, "I can't!"

"Why not?"

"I don't have my parachute on!"

I was feeling a little airsick and bleeding from a gash in my shoulder, but I just could not leave Ben alone and without a chute. He would run out of altitude before he could put it on.

I made my way forward and noticed that my pistol had fallen on the floor. I picked it up and returned it to its holster.

This particular glider used a single control column. To transfer control from pilot to co-pilot required pulling a pin and pivoting the column to the co-pilot's side. It was impossible to even attempt to transfer the controls.

However, we were lucky. Below us was a good-sized dry lake.

I cut the glider loose from the towline, and told Ben my plan regarding the lake bed. He would have to handle the landing. There was a tremendous force acting against the control column, and he told me that we would have to fly at an airspeed of 120 mph, just to keep the ship under control. I sat down in the co-pilot's seat once again and told Ben that I would apply spoilers according to his instructions.

We were losing altitude fast. As we hurtled towards the earth, Ben lined the glider up with the dry lake. A minute later, we slammed down doing 125 mph. Ben released the controls and we came to a bumpy stop.

The first thing Ben did was to take his pants down and lose all control of his bowels through the gaping hole in the floor. It had been an unnerving experience, but my mind had now moved on to something else.

"Hey Ben," I said, "what are we going to do? We're about a hundred miles from nowhere. In case we meet up with unfriendly Arabs, I only have seven rounds of ammo."

"Forget the gun," Ben replied. "We'll just have to cooperate with them."

I decided to lie down in the shade of the glider's wing. I used my parachute as a pillow and took a snooze. I had just gotten into a relaxing nap, when I heard the tick-tick-ticking of two aircraft engines. The DC-3 must have been close by, because the sound of the engines idling was quite loud. Then I heard a voice.

"You want a ride, Bagley?"

It was Tom Crause! He was risking his life for us two downed glider pilots.

After the DC-3 lifted off, Tom headed eastward for Oujda. The only items we salvaged from the CG-4A were my .45-caliber revolver, my beloved sweater, the glider's radio and first aid kit and our parachutes. I noticed that Ben was now wearing his.

When we arrived over the base in Oujda, we were shocked by what we saw. Our gliders were completely demolished—all sixty of them! Some tents were also destroyed, but all 100 DC-3s were undamaged. Tom landed and taxied to the 49th Squadron tie-down area. I rushed over to Group Engineering, and found out that several groups in the area had also lost all their gliders. The gliders had been secured using a standard six-point tie-down, and all control surfaces had been provided with a lock. Spoilers were attached to all glider wings. In spite of all these precautions, we lost hundreds of gliders due to the vicious line squalls in the area.

I issued the following order (Group Order 7) to all Squadron Glider Engineering Officers:

In the future, all tie-downs are to be 12-point.

A fifty-pound cement block is to be buried under each tie-down location, and all glider wings secured to it with a steel cable.

All gliders are to be parked with their tails into the wind.

The next day I was ordered to be the "Officer of the Day," responsible for security and guard duty for the 49th's assigned area. I was issued a jeep and driver, a sergeant of the guard and one dozen guards. I had the driver take me on a tour of our area, just to look things over. We came to a field in which a POW was working. No one had ever mentioned to me that we had any Italian POWs in the area. I wondered why there were no guards around, as the POW was close to one of our DC-3s. I decided that I was not going to take any chances. I ordered him aboard the jeep, and we drove to Group Headquarters. I told the sergeant to keep an eye on him until I returned. I went directly to the adjutant, and asked him if he knew of any POWs working on the base.

"Yes of course," he replied. "There are about two dozen assigned to do the gardening around our camp."

As long as he was aware of the situation, I told my driver to go ahead and return the POW to his original location. I wasn't feeling all that great, and asked the driver next to take me over to the Flight Surgeon's office. I went directly into his tent, sat down, and said, "Major, I don't feel well!"

Then everything went black. No sound, either. I would have guessed I was out for only a few seconds, but I awoke in a strange place. I thought that I was dreaming . . . or maybe dead. A pretty lady in soft green came over to me and said, "Oh, I see you're awake."

I asked, "Where am I?"

She answered, "In a hospital; in Casablanca."

I asked how long I had been there. "Three days," she replied.

"But how did I get here?"

"Tom Crause flew you down from Oujda in an air ambulance. He asked us to take good care of you."

Then I asked her what was wrong with me. She said that I had an extremely high fever, and that it caused me to slip into unconsciousness. She then asked me to get up and walk, that it would be the best thing to speed my recovery. My temperature was normal and in another three days, I was dressed and walking around the hospital grounds.

That day, a pleasant-looking Arab boy about ten years old came up to me and asked, "Need a shine, mister?" I looked down at my shoes, and said, "OK."

When he finished, I asked him how much I owed him. He thought for a moment, and said, "Three francs." I handed him the coins, and he said, "Thanks, mister!"

As I walked away, I saw a very well-dressed older boy come over to him and hold out his hand. The younger boy handed over his hard-earned three francs. After the two of them separated, I followed the boy who had shined my shoes.

I eventually caught up with him and handed him fifty francs. "Look, kid, go out and buy your own shoeshine kit. This money is for you, understand?" He smiled and nodded, "Yes." Then I walked back to the hospital. They told me I would be discharged in two more days.

❖   ❖   ❖

On Friday, July 9, 1943, I checked the bulletin board, and learned that my name was listed on flying orders for the Sicily invasion. Takeoff time was set for 0600 on Saturday, July 10. Our landing zone was on the coast at the southeast tip of Sicily, in the area of Syracuse. We were to move in and hold existing bridges.

Flight Officer Franklin came to see me at Group Engineering. He told me he was disappointed that he was not listed on the flying orders for the invasion, and asked if he could go in my place.

"Franklin," I said, "that's not the way it works. Squadron Ops have made their selections and posted the flying orders. I don't have the authority to make changes!"

"OK," Franklin admitted. "But would you mind if I went in your place?"

"No, I would not mind, but I think you're nuts! I'm not going anywhere near operations to request any change to their original selection. If you must, go ahead and talk to Lt. Hamilton. He may add you to the list."

About an hour later, Franklin rushed into my office and announced that he was going in my place; the order had been changed.

The next morning at 0600 I watched as half of our gliders lifted off from the Oujda air base for the invasion of Sicily. After the gliders lifted off, the balance of fifty DC-3s took off with paratroopers heading for their designated drop zones.

At 1000 we spotted several of the DC-3s coming back. After arriving overhead, they peeled off, landing on runway 18. By 1100, six more had come in, landing in single file. By noon the last few stragglers (those who sustained the most damage) came limping home, some on one engine. We estimated a fifteen percent loss of planes and crews. All the losses inflicted upon the 313th that day were due to U.S. Navy friendly fire, not the enemy.

I knew that our CO was leading the paratroop formation, and that Tom Crause was his co-pilot. I met up with Tom at lunch and asked him how everything went.

Tom explained that as they were heading north out of Tunis, they came upon a huge fleet of ships. The invading armada was also on a northern heading for the southern tip of Italy. The air became full of antiaircraft fire; tow planes were going down, their gliders crashing into the sea. Tom said that even though he could see men being pulled aboard, the antiaircraft fire did not let up. From this point on, the situation went from SNAFU to TARFU. Many gliders released prematurely and did not have sufficient altitude to reach their landing zones. Only a handful of gliders ever reached their objectives.

Tom went on to say that after passing over the flotilla of ships, he and his crew crossed the shoreline and proceeded to their designated drop zone, where they unloaded their paratroopers. When flying back over the armada, they again were met with intense fire.

He exclaimed, "The ships had us mixed up with the German twin-engine bombers, about the same size and shape as our DC-3s! The Colonel had both throttles pushed all the way to the firewall. When I reached over to pull them back, he slapped my wrist, saying 'Don't fuck with the throttles, Tom!'

"I answered, 'But Sir, you're going to burn out those engines!'

'The hell with the engines,' he said, 'we're getting out of here, NOW!'"

Tom then told us of how the Colonel quickly outlined his plan for getting through the deadly gunfire.

"'We are now at 3,000 feet. I'm going to dive down at 300 mph and level off at three to four feet above the water. We're gonna fly in between the ships, so that we are below their decks. If they continue to fire at us as we pass by, they will be caught in their own crossfire!'"

Tom explained triumphantly, "We put his plan to the test. The ships stopped firing at us as we went by, and we headed for home!"

❧   ❧   ❧

Over the next ten days, glider pilots from the 49th made their way back to Oujda a few at a time. Upon his return, I was happy to see Flight Officer Franklin. I asked him what his experience was like.

"My tow plane was shot down as we approached our landing zone," he told me. "I found myself in free flight, with insufficient altitude to make landfall. I had to swim a quarter mile to shore."

I told him, "Franklin, being a good swimmer saved your life! If I had flown that mission, I probably wouldn't be here talking to you. I couldn't swim in boot camp . . . and I can't swim now!"

A day or two later, I was walking past the Major's office, when I recognized his all-too-familiar summons. "Bagley! Step into my office."

I rendered a salute, which he acknowledged, saying, "I have in my possession a bill from the United States Treasury for $2.75. It's from an overpayment to you when you were discharged as a staff sergeant in Kansas City. This is your second notice and I suggest you pay it. Take this to Captain Hickman in the finance office and ask him to take care of the details."

"Yes, Sir." I replied. "I'll handle it right away."

Captain Hickman had it deducted from my pay. As I was leaving the orderly room, I noticed we had a new feature film that was showing that night, *Arsenic and Old Lace*. Mary had written about it to me. She said that when she saw it in a theatre in Hollywood, she laughed so hard that everyone was looking at her instead of the movie.

The movie viewing equipment provided to each squadron consisted of a 35mm projector, audio speakers and an electric generator. The "theatre" consisted of selecting a flat area on the sand (for the screen) and hooking up the generator. We tried to find the longest extension cord there was, so that the noise from the generator would not interfere with the sound from the speakers. All moviegoers had to bring their own "box seat" (a crate to sit on), or just sit on the ground.

Our feature films usually ran over long periods, like thirty days. We saw *Lincoln in Illinois* every night for a month. By the time we got a new movie, we could perfectly recite every line of the old one.

Arsenic and Old Lace drew a crowd for about two weeks running. Pilots and co-pilots alike would yell, "Chaaarge!" as they ran up "San Juan Hill," the ramp of their DC-3, to their seats.

❖   ❖   ❖

One morning before dawn, I awoke needing to empty my bladder. I picked up my .45 automatic and headed for one of our urinals. Our urinals consisted of a two-inch pipe, about three-feet long, coming out of the ground. The top of the pipe had a concrete funnel, which we called the Berlin Telephone Network Listening Post.

As I returned to my bunk, I felt the unmistakable bite of a gun barrel pressed into my back.

"Is that you, Bagley?"

"Yes, it's me, Tom," I answered. "Who the hell do you think it is?"

At that moment, I heard the drone of approaching aircraft. We had been told earlier that the Germans were planning to drop paratroopers in our area. Now, we saw several airplanes, with paratroopers jumping out at about 400 feet above us.

I took careful aim at a solider coming in directly ahead. Just as I was starting to squeeze the trigger, the planes turned on their identification lights. It was another U.S. AAF squadron. They were playing war games and claimed this "air raid" as a victory. I wondered what kind of idiot would play war games in a real war zone, especially when we just lost fifteen percent of our planes and crews to friendly fire! I was damn mad, because I came within a microsecond of killing a paratrooper; it might have been Dominic or his CO who just came to Oujda to visit me a few weeks ago.

❖   ❖   ❖

One morning, I decided that it was going to be my day to do whatever I wanted. After breakfast, I went over to the kitchen tent and spoke to the cook. I asked him if I could use the kitchen for a while, because I wanted to make apple turnovers. I was surprised when he said yes. I asked him for the following: a cookie sheet, rolling pin, flour, shortening, sugar, salt, cinnamon, nutmeg and ground allspice.

"I have all but the rolling pin and the allspice," he replied.

"Oh yeah," he added. "No apples."

"How about applesauce?" I asked. Yes, he had plenty of that.

I had seen my mother make apple turnovers and cinnamon rolls, and had memorized the whole procedure. I cut in the shortening until the flour mixture was the size of small peas. I found a bottle and used it for a rolling pin. I trimmed the dough to its proper size, adding a little flour and cornstarch to the applesauce to thicken it up. I put it in a 375° oven until it browned. While they were still hot, I put a little sugar on them, and when they cooled off, I wrapped them in aluminum foil. I had eight delicious-looking apple turnovers, which I placed in a homemade screen box to keep the flies off. I put the box in my tent for safekeeping.

When I left my tent, I heard the sound of a twin-engine approaching our base from the south. There was a British air base located ten miles south of us, and whenever the wind was from the north, they would climb out over our base on their way to bomb targets in Italy and Sicily. Their planes were Wellington light bombers, with a two-man crew. They could carry around five or six 500-pound bombs. I was just beyond the end of runway 36 when I saw the Wellington at about 1,500 feet. His engines were failing—and his bomb bay doors were open. I saw a bomb drop; it was in free flight directly overhead. I tried to determine in which direction it was falling. Luckily, it seemed to be moving northward. If I could not discern the direction of its fall, it would land on the very spot where I was standing. I looked up to see another bomb leave the bay. I figured I was safe, as both of them would land north of the base in the open desert.

The Wellington (nicknamed a "Wimpy") was circling back at 600 feet. Both engines had died, and his landing gear was not down. They were making a belly landing with live bombs on board. I prayed the plane would not explode on impact. Thankfully, it touched down and skidded to a stop about 600 feet from where I was standing. I ran as quickly as I could to help them both out. They yelled that I had better get away from there fast, it might explode any second.

Both the pilot and co-pilot were uninjured, but were very shaken up after their ordeal. When we were safely away from the downed aircraft, I asked why the bombs had not exploded on impact. They explained that they were all delayed-action bombs and would explode in a random manner, including the four left in the bomb bay.

The Officer of the Day came by in his jeep and we explained to him that the area of the plane was very dangerous. It was imperative that no one go near it. I then asked him to take the British pilots to our mess hall for a hot cup of coffee, and to arrange transportation for them back to their base.

About an hour later, the Wellington blew up. The fuel had ignited, causing the bombs left on board to detonate.

We received word that we were to evacuate our base the following day at 1200 hours. Around 1700, a violent hurricane moved in to our area. It was a line squall type of thunderstorm, with winds of 70-80 mph and hail. At 1800, the storm was still raging. It was pitch dark. The other two bombs that the Wellington dropped in the desert exploded, adding to the chaos of thunder and lightning filling the air. I saw one of our gliders in free flight, spinning like a cartwheel, with its two, fifty-pound cement blocks still attached to the wing struts. It crashed down on our kitchen tent, where just that morning I had made my apple turnovers. Luckily, no one was in it at the time.

The storm lasted another two hours. When it was over, we took inventory. The 49th and 29th Squadrons had each lost one glider. No DC-3s were destroyed.

Wing Command called up to ask us for a group status report, and I reported the loss of the two gliders. They were convinced that we did not get the brunt of the storm.

"Oh yes, we did!" I assured them. "We had two gliders flying around, despite the two fifty-pound blocks I ordered them tied down to. These blocks were buried two feet underground and got pulled out. This is in addition to the twelve-point tie-down that I ordered."

They couldn't believe it, because other groups had reported losses of twenty to thirty gliders apiece.

At high noon the next day, we departed Oujda for good. I put my apple turnovers in my knapsack, and draped it over the back of my seat in the glider. I was piloting the last glider to leave the air base.

We were to land in Tunis for refreshments, then proceed on to Sicily. Looking down at the runway in Tunis, I saw it crowded with DC-3s. They were lined up on each side, with only fifty or sixty feet between wing tips. I had to decide quickly whether landing there was possible or not. I figured that my glider's wings would clear theirs by one and a half to two feet vertically. In other words, my wings would be slightly higher and I'd manage to pass over them. I also had to quickly estimate if my wing tips would clear their propellers. I figured

I could clear them by four to five feet on each side. I squeezed by and landed on that runway, with transports lining both sides.

As it turns out, it wasn't worth it. There were no refreshments in Tunis and we had nothing for dinner or breakfast the next morning.

At 1000 hours I was sitting in my glider, ready to takeoff for Sicily. My co-pilot was Flight Officer Barnes. Our tow plane taxied into position, and the ground crew connected our towline and interphone. I called the tow plane pilot and told him we were ready. Halfway down the runway we were airborne, headed for our destination of Marsala, Italy. We were soon over the bright blue Mediterranean Sea. It looked so peaceful and relaxing.

I asked Barnes, "When did you eat last?"

He said, "About two days ago."

I said, "Gee, I remember my mom made the best apple turnovers. I'd sure like to have one or two of them now. They sure smelled good coming out of the oven . . . the best I ever tasted!"

"Bagley, I'm so hungry. Shut the hell up about apple turnovers!"

"Barnes, look in my knapsack. I have apple turnovers, I really do."

"Quit dreaming and be quiet."

He wouldn't buy it, so I reached into my knapsack and took out the foil-wrapped packages. I handed two to Barnes, telling him to enjoy. We each had two on our way to Sicily. It was late August 1943.

Chapter 8
PREPARING FOR INVASION
The island of Sicily

Barnes and I were flying due north at 7,000 feet. Upon reaching the island of Sicily, we turned northwest, passed over the town of Gila and continued along the coastline to the town of Marsala, our new home. The tow plane pilot called on the interphone and advised us that after dropping the towrope alongside, he would be landing runway 36.

"Roger, tow plane," I answered. "I'll be number two to land runway 36 and cast off."

I circled the field several times, and was surprised at all the German ME-109s parked in cement revetments. There were at least a dozen and at first glance, they appeared to be in good shape. I wondered, if this had been an active German airfield, why didn't they take their ME-109s with them? I found out later that they had ultimately run out of fuel. Instead of letting them fall into enemy hands, the Germans decided to sabotage the planes.

To me, the Germans' efforts seemed illogical. They should have destroyed all the control panels, or all the propellers. Instead, they had destroyed each of them in a random manner. I estimated that by cannibalization of parts, I could have one up and running in two weeks' time. These particular ME-109s were built in 1943 and had the following characteristics:

Power plant:	Built by Daimler-Benz
Horsepower:	1,150 at takeoff
Airspeed:	398 mph max, 365 cruising
Engine:	Liquid-cooled inverted V-12 with fuel injection
Ceiling:	36,000 feet

I contacted Flight Officer Cuthbertson, the 49th Squadron Glider Engineering Officer, and Captain Bailey, Glider Engineering Officer for the 29th Troop Carrier Squadron. They were both interested in restoring an ME-109.

We chose one we thought would be a good candidate to return to air-worthiness, and ended up replacing a cylinder on the engine, an aileron and patching the wing. In doing so, we discovered the ME-109 had many desirable features that our aircraft lacked. For example, if a German pilot found his engine badly damaged, but could make it back to his airfield, he could land, taxi to the repair shop and go have a cup of coffee in the mess hall. When he got back to his plane, he would find a new engine installed. They could change out an engine in fifteen or twenty minutes. To change an engine on a DC-3, we needed three days.

We found that the ME-109s had quick-disconnect fittings. The oil, coolant and hydraulic lines, electrical connections, instrumentation lines and special engine mounts were easy for mechanics to connect and disconnect. There were two-inch, union-connected motor mounts, the last thing to be disconnected during engine replacement.

Precision ball bearing pulleys were employed on all aileron, elevator and rudder controls. Only a few ounces of torque were required to operate any on-board controls. You could move the elevator controls with your little finger.

The other officers and I took turns taxiing the ME-109 along the runway. We tried to get permission to fly the plane around our airfield, but Colonel Roberts wanted no part of it. Eventually, it got back to General Eisenhower that we had restored an ME-109. He ordered our sub depot at Ponte-Olevio to ship the aircraft to Wright-Patterson field in Ohio for evaluation. The sub depot also picked up all of the remaining ME-109s. I was left with the feeling that in this man's Army, glider pilots were destined to fly only gliders, and so it went.

❄   ❄   ❄

One morning, as I was coming out of the mess hall, I noticed that our glider crew chiefs had all been issued bicycles. They were heading toward our flight line at an extremely rapid pace. I thought, these guys can't all be in that much of a hurry to get to work. So, I walked down there to see what the big attraction was. I could no longer see any bicycles, and everyone had vanished.

110

Perplexed, I walked over to the motor pool, where Bob Piser issued me a jeep and driver. I felt sorry for my old friend Bob. He had ruined his career in the Army through too much gambling and had been demoted to running the motor pool instead of being the 49th Squadron Engineering Officer.

I explained to my driver what I had seen, and asked, "Sergeant, do you have any idea where they are?" He told me that yes, he did. There was a house of prostitution about a mile from camp, and he suggested that we look there.

When we reached our destination, sure enough, eighteen bicycles were parked on various sides of the house.

I told the driver, "Sergeant, you had better come with me—I might need your help."

I turned the knob on the front door and found it locked. I kicked it in and went to every room, whether it was open or closed. Throughout the house I repeated in a loud voice, "Soldiers, don't be surprised if you get back to camp and find yourselves arrested for being AWOL!" Then I returned to the jeep, telling the driver, "Let's get the hell out of here!"

About an hour later I walked down to the flight line. I had the sergeant in charge assemble the men and bring them to attention. I put them at ease and said something like, "As glider crew chiefs, you have perhaps the softest and safest job in the entire Air Force. You never have to fly a mission or worry about being shot at. You always have the best food—the same as officers. All you have to do is to keep these gliders in tip-top shape. I expect you to be doing your job between the hours of 0800 and 1700, unless of course you have a valid pass to be elsewhere. This morning, many of you were AWOL from this base, which is a court-martial offense. If any of you are arrested and found guilty, I am going to recommend that you be given a choice between a court-martial sentence or a transfer to the 82nd Airborne infantry. If you should request a transfer, all court-martial charges against you will be deleted. My suggestion is that you never again leave camp without a pass.

"Do I have to ask the question, 'Is my message coming through loud and clear?' Hell no! I know damn well it is! And do I have to ask, 'Do you understand what I'm trying to say?' Hell no! I know you do! You are dismissed."

I turned on my heels and headed back to the group engineering office. As I was walking towards headquarters, I noticed two Horsa gliders in free flight preparing for a landing on runway 36. Compared to our CG-4As, they were huge. The first one made a good landing and rolled along the taxiway toward the 49th Squadron apron. The second glider made a good touchdown on its rear wheels, but when the nose wheel came down, it disappeared into the fuselage. The entire nose section was rubbing along the runway. The pilot braked, using the rear wheels. Applying right or left wheel braking was the only way he had to control the glider's direction; using left brake to go left, right brake to go to the right. Using the rudder had no effect because the pivoting front wheel was stuck and could not function.

Shortly after the Horsa came to a stop, I ran over to it and climbed aboard. I was completely shocked by what I found in the cockpit. I complimented the pilot, Flight Officer Landel, on his exceptional flying skills. He had had no rudder control; his only method of directional control was to use the brakes. When that nose wheel came up through the floor, it was rotating at a speed of 1,000 revolutions per minute. Like a giant Skilsaw, it spit sharp wood chips, sawdust and other debris like shrapnel, blinding both pilots. They were lucky to be alive. I again asked them if they were OK. They both said yes, they were, so I asked Landel to hand me the glider's logbook. I made the entry, "This glider is not to be repaired, but destroyed."

I instructed the ground crew to take the remaining Horsa glider over to the 49th Squadron tie down area and put it on a warm-up pad on runway 36 for a 0900 takeoff. I was going to test it the next day, and Tom Crouse was going to fly the tow plane. I alerted the ground crew, reminding them not to forget about the three connections required to tow a Horsa.

The next morning we were ready to roll on runway 36. I asked Tom to make the takeoff slow and gradual. In order to test the glider, I would need to be towed at about 125 mph, but no faster. Once at the proper speed, I decided to check out the glider's rudder. I gave it a little bit of right rudder and it immediately opened up a huge seam on the left side of the glider. When I gave it a little left rudder, it opened a big seam on the right side.

I told Tom, "I'm in trouble! To hell with doing any more testing. If I can get this bird back on terra firma, it's grounded!" I decided to ask Tom to tow me out to the far end of runway 36 where I would try to come in at a 1,000-foot elevation, straight-in approach.

I told him, "I'm going to have to fly it in all the way. Once I get it down to the right speed, the Horsa will fall out of the sky and the three wheels will touch automatically. I'll cut off when I feel I am at the right altitude to attempt the landing. Thanks for the ride, Tom!"

When we got about a half mile from the end of runway 36, I cut loose from the tow and let the Horsa glide using aileron and elevator control only. Once the airspeed dropped to about 60 mph, I pulled back on the control column, slowing it down even more. Even though the glider was ripped open like a can of sardines, I made a perfect three-point landing, all three wheels touching down at the same time. I let the glider coast down the runway and used the brakes to bring the plane to rest at the end of the field.

I took out my logbook and made the entry, "This glider is to be destroyed."

The next day I filed the status report on the second glider to be demolished and other Horsas to be grounded. Wing was mad as hell when they found out I was ordering two Horsa gliders destroyed and others grounded. They questioned my authority as to ground any gliders, or to have them destroyed for that matter. Wing wanted to use the Horsas as training gliders for the Americans while we were teaching the British how to fly CG-4As.

About 0900 the following day, a bright and shiny new DC-3 arrived, and Major Bailey got out. He wanted to know who had grounded the Horsa gliders. I said, "I did, Sir. When I took one for a test flight it began to fall apart. We were damn lucky to get out of it alive."

"Well", he said, "I think we should give it another flight test."

I informed him of the problem I had encountered with the Horsa, and described the five-to-six-foot-long tear down both sides of the fuselage. I strongly recommended against taking a test flight, but he insisted.

With much reservation, I said, "OK."

We got the crew chiefs and the glider back on the runway. I proceeded to tell Major Bailey exactly what would happen.

"We are going up in a glider but we are coming back in a parachute. If that's what you want, I will take you, but my wife and your wife will not be eligible for any life insurance should we crash during the test flight. We have not been given orders to fly Horsa gliders that have been scheduled for destruction. And another thing, Major, when you bail out of a glider it is not like bailing out of an airplane. The glider does not speed away from you at 300 mph, as a conventional plane would do. It stays overhead. That means that if we jump at say, 5,000 feet, we need to descend to at least 3,000 feet to get away from the glider. If any part of it comes in contact with your parachute, you will not live to tell about it. If that's what you want to do, let's go!"

Major Bailey pondered this scenario for a moment and said, "Uh, OK . . . I think you're right about the Horsas."

"Alright," I said, "but don't ever send me any more of them."

He promised he wouldn't.

The next morning I met up with Tom. He asked me if I would like to go into Palermo with him to see the sights. I told him yes, definitely. I thought we were going to the motor pool to get a jeep, but instead we went down to the line and got into a DC-3. Another officer by the name of Max Becker was also there. He had been promoted from flight officer to lieutenant. On this particular flight, the crew was Tom, the pilot, the copilot, Becker, and me.

We had to approach Palermo from the south because of the barrage balloons. These balloons were stationary, tethered by steel cables. They floated at 2,000 to 3,000 feet in the air above the city and could rip any plane in half that tried to fly in. Only a very experienced pilot would dare attempt it. The only way to land was a straight-in approach through a canyon. I heard Tom say over the radio, "We are about five miles to touchdown and in line with the runway."

Suddenly, as we were coming through the canyon, there was a severe updraft. Becker, the corpse and I all went up to the ceiling and were floating around the cabin, much as the astronauts do in space. Then we came down with a crash. In fact, I hurt my back when I plummeted down, falling right on the corner of a bench. It was extremely painful, and I was not sure I could move. When I did attempt to move, I found that I was wearing Becker's helmet and he was wearing mine! When I finally was able to get up, I went over the left side of the plane and looked out the window. I saw in amazement that at least twenty feet of the left wing had been sheared off.

Becker said, "I guess we must have hit the canyon."

"No," I said, "if we had hit the canyon we would have cartwheeled, and that would have been the end of us. It was wind shear."

Tom was struggling to get the DC-3 under control, but it was not responding. At any moment, I expected him to order the Crew Chief to open the emergency doors in preparation for a crash landing. I could not understand why he hadn't. Tom was a masterful pilot, but I was not sure if he could get us out of this alive. When he put the flaps down, I knew the runway must be in sight. We were coming in fast, at least 120 mph. Tom somehow managed to get the DC-3 back under control; the field was coming up fast. When the wheels touched down, we all breathed a sigh of relief. We rolled to a stop at the end of the field and got out. After inspecting the sheared off wing, we agreed we were all very lucky to be back on solid ground, thanks to Tom Crouse.

When I got the opportunity to talk to Tom in private, I asked him why he had not ordered the Crew Chief to open the emergency doors. He said, "When I received my first DC-3 and we were on a routine flight, an alarm indicated a fire in the number two engine. I ordered the Crew Chief to open all the emergency doors. When he opened the main cargo door, he got sucked out of the plane along with the door. I followed him all the way down. He was still clutching the door handle when he hit the ground. I marked the location on my navigation chart so that his body could be retrieved later. Needless to say, I have never given that order again."

By this time, we had to cancel our sightseeing plans in Palermo. We waited for the pick-up plane to arrive, then headed back to our base, praying for an uneventful flight.

❖   ❖   ❖

General Patton wanted us to put on a demonstration for him, and he wanted this demonstration to be performed at the airport in Comiso. He wanted us to fly in a battalion and some artillery pieces to the south side of the airport. Then, at first light, the paratroopers would simulate an attack on the airport, followed by the infantry. Patton wanted us to give him a realistic demonstration of what an attack on the airport would look like. The demonstration was to take place in just over one week.

My job was to fly in with one of the jeeps and four soldiers as cargo. The jeep would pull the artillery piece being transported by another glider, also carrying four soldiers. We were to land on one of two fields that were just south of the airport. The fields were approximately 500 feet below the main airfield.

I was the first one to cut loose from the tow plane. I spotted the small field below the main airport where I was to land, but there was a problem; two teams of horses were plowing the field. Every time I lined up for a landing, the horses were in the path of my glider. I had

115

to change course about three times and maintain enough airspeed to land farther down the field, before finally evading them. Just as I was about to land, I saw a bicycle right where I had planned to put down. I didn't want to wreck it, so I pulled up, but was now heading right for an irrigation ditch. Luckily, the ditch had a little embankment that gave enough lift to keep me off the ground.

I had jettisoned my gear earlier and unlocked the nose; otherwise, the jeep could crush me to death on impact. Having missed two teams of horses, a bicycle and an irrigation ditch, I was not surprised when I saw what looked to be an outhouse dead ahead. It was painted white, with a red window shaped like a half moon. I had no more airspeed and had to land the glider even though I might take out the outhouse in the process. Just before I reached it, the door flew open and out ran a man, holding up his pants, headed for the woods.

As soon as I managed to land, the jeep was driven out of the glider and over to pick up the artillery from the other glider. General Patton rolled up in his tank, looked in the door of my glider and asked, "Where's the jeep?"

I said, "It went to pick up the gun."

"Oh," he said. "Good flying!"

I think the demonstration impressed him.

❖   ❖   ❖

Doc Ott, three other officers and I decided we would take a ride up to Mt. Erice and make a contribution to the orphanage that stood at its summit. We took cheese, canned fruit and flour. Such things were in short supply there. We loaded them in the jeep and headed up the mountain, which overlooks the town of Trapani on the northwest coast of Sicily.

When we got to the top, about 2,400 feet, I noticed there were strong updrafts. There were hundreds of birds, some ridge soaring, some floating up and down with the air currents and others doing acrobatics. I was fascinated and spent about ten minutes watching them. The other guys wondered what my preoccupation was with those birds.

"Hey, Bagley, let's get inside," one of the guys finally called out.

We went in the front door and unloaded our food for the children. We could tell how grateful they were. There were about twenty orphans in all. We asked one of the nuns in charge if we could look around, and she said we could.

We opened a door that looked like the entrance to a bunker and were amazed at what we found. We had stumbled on to a German torpedo factory, complete with a machine shop located inside the mountain. It had suspended rooms containing welders, lathes and drill press tools. There were dozens and dozens of torpedoes stacked neatly against the walls.

Suddenly, I felt a chill run down my spine. A little voice in my head said, "Get the hell out of here, this place might be booby trapped!"

The Germans had been known to booby trap an installation before leaving, and they were long gone. I called to the men, "Be very careful. Try to retrace your steps to the outside as quickly as you can. I suspect that this place may be wired to explode and if it goes off, the whole top of the mountain is going with it. Let's do our best to get out of here alive."

We went out single file, retracing our steps as best we could. We thought every step might be our last. We told the nuns what we had found and that we would report this to command headquarters, which would follow up with demolition experts that could safely destroy the factory.

The next day, I had a routine flight scheduled for all glider pilots. I took off at 0900 in a CG-4A. Tom Crouse was flying the tow plane. Ordinarily, he would take me to 3,000 feet, and I would cut loose. I usually made a few maneuvers before heading back to the field for a landing. But this day I asked Tom to take me to 7,000 feet. He asked, "Why?"

I said, "I would like to head over to Mt. Erice to do some ridge soaring and I need enough altitude to make it back."

"Okay," he said.

At 7,000 feet, I cut loose and headed for the mountain. I remembered those birds I had seen there, and I wanted to see what I could do in a glider. I ran into terrifically strong updrafts that quickly took me from 5,000 feet back up to 7,000 feet. It was like being in an elevator. By watching the birds soaring I could see where the strongest updrafts were and I was able to stay aloft for several hours. I could have stayed up much longer, but a couple of the guys who were with me said they needed to use the bathroom and asked if I would take them back to the field. I landed the glider and when I went to log in the flight time, I found I had been up four and one-half hours. I did not think that a CG-4A could do that. It had a lot of drag, but got a lot of lift from those strong updrafts. I was able to fly the glider as a sailplane. I would advise any pilot who would like to set an endurance record in a sailplane to head for Mt. Erice.

❀   ❀   ❀

It was 2200 and four gliders were coming in under tow. They unhooked their towlines as four DC-3s flew overhead. The gliders were on their final approach to runway 36 and all was well, until a stray C-47 came taxiing down the runway. It was headed the wrong way and had its landing lights on. Meanwhile, the bright lights of the C-47 were blinding the glider pilots and it was too late to abort their landing.

The C-47 turned off the runway, but not soon enough to avoid disaster. One of gliders hit the ground so hard it bounced thirty feet into the air before crashing back down again. Another glider crashed into a revetment and was all but destroyed. The two other two gliders met with a similar fate.

The C-47 taxied over to where I was standing and parked. I could not believe what had just happened. I ripped the C-47's door open and charged up the aisle, swearing all the way to the cockpit. I was furious and let loose with a tirade.

"You stupid bastards, what the hell do you think you are doing? You're taxiing down an active runway going the wrong way. I think you just killed everyone onboard those gliders. What do you have to say for yourselves?"

I soon realized what the problem was. Neither man at the controls of the C-47 was a pilot. They were both crew chiefs, and drunk as skunks. I could not believe what I was seeing! I ordered them to shut down the engines at once and to give me the keys.

Then one of them said, "I can't do that. I can't do that."

I replied, "You better do it, or I will place you under arrest. If I have to tell you a second time, I will shoot you!"

The guy decided I was serious. He shut down the engines and handed me the keys to the plane. I stormed out of the cockpit, still mad as hell.

The CO would decide what to do with the drunken crew chiefs later; for now, I had to check on the status of the glider pilots and crew. I found out that four men had broken legs and the rest had other serious injuries, but there were no fatalities. That was a miracle. We flew the injured to one of the best military hospitals for treatment, which happened to be in Casablanca.

The next day the crew chiefs' CO asked me if I had the keys to his airplane. I said, "Yes, sir. I found two drunks taxiing the wrong way on an active runway. They could have killed our glider pilots and crew. I think we should have Group talk to Colonel Roberts and have him issue an order to this effect: 'From this date forward no crew chiefs are allowed to taxi airplanes, only licensed pilots can taxi aircraft.'"

That rule was put into effect as a result of this incident. Hopefully, it prevented anything like this from ever happening again.

Later, I was given the task of investigating another glider crash, and correcting the cause.

One of our gliders had been on tow and it went into a series of outside loops. Luckily, the pilots were able to bail out after cutting loose from the tow plane. The glider crashed when the towline became wrapped around a telephone pole. Because the towline was attached to the nose, the glider was pulled right into the ground, smashing it to smithereens.

So, I went through the rubble bit by bit, looking for a piece of wood with a round hole in it. A brace wire goes out from the horizontal stabilizer to the vertical fin that holds the rudderpost. I theorized that if I could find the bolt for the rudderpost, I could identify the problem. I sifted through lots of rubble looking for that bolt and anything that might prove my theory wrong.

None of the tail fittings was damaged. Finally, I came to a piece of wood with a perfectly round hole in it. A bolt had dislodged from the rudderpost, leaving a round hole. Experience told me that if the bolt had been intact at the time of the crash, the hole would have been splintered and not perfectly round, because the bolt would have been ripped out by the force of the crash. All I needed to do now was to find the bolt.

After about three hours of searching, I found what I had been looking for. It had become brittle in the center, and split in two. The broken bolt had pulled out from either side of the rudderpost, causing the glider to go into outside loops.

After discovering the problem, I proceeded to ground all 100 gliders. I knew I would have some explaining to do. My CO called me in, wanting to know why I had grounded the gliders.

I said, "Sir, I found the culprit. A bolt." I explained to him in detail what I had found. "We have to look at every one of these bolts on all 100 gliders. I am ordering the crew chiefs to remove the bolt from the rudderpost in all of them. We will need to send the bolts to our sub-depot in Ponte Olivo for magnifluxing. Those bolts that are found to be in good condition will be reinstalled in the gliders. If any of the bolts need to be replaced, those gliders will remain grounded. If we start right away, we should be able to get the fleet back in operation within forty-eight hours."

After having all the bolts magnifluxed, we only found three defective bolts; thus, only three gliders remained grounded. As a result of my investigation, future accidents of this nature had been averted.

❖   ❖   ❖

We had about 100 gliders lined up behind tow planes ready to take off for our support role in the Battle of Salerno.

We all went into the briefing room, where a captain showed us some pictures of mountains, snowfields and areas designated as drop zones for paratroopers and landing zones for gliders. The Captain began describing in detail where the gliders could land, indicating that up to twenty gliders could be put down in one field alone. Then he pointed to another area that he described as a long landing field, ideal for gliders.

"We will be taking off in about twenty minutes," he said.

I took a good look at the pictures, and noted that they had been taken early in the morning. That's when it struck me that the briefing officer had missed a critical point, and was about to send us on a suicide mission.

I went outside, my mind racing frantically, trying to figure out what to do. I was cursing in frustration when a captain, who was also a chaplain, approached, and asked me what was wrong. I told him about the briefing and the pictures we had been shown of fields supposedly safe for landing gliders and paratroopers.

I explained to him that what the briefing officer described as a landing site was actually the sheer face of a cliff. In addition, what he thought was a landing zone was really a mountain casting a shadow.

120

Being an experienced pilot, I was able to recognize the difference. I explained to that there actually were no landing zones for gliders or paratroopers within miles of that area.

He thanked me for the information and disappeared into the briefing room.

Once the order was given, the DC-3 pilots began to warm up their engines, ready for the mission. But a few minutes after the Captain entered the briefing room, all the engines shut down and the runway fell silent. The mission had been scrapped. I got out of my glider and went back to my room. No explanation was given as to why the mission had been called off. Only I knew the real reason.

❖   ❖   ❖

My copilot and I were on takeoff with a "green" tow-plane pilot. It was the first time he had ever towed a glider. We took off in the normal fashion; I was about fifty feet above and behind the DC-3 when my towline came loose and broke. Instead of getting out of the way, the inexperienced pilot started to slow down, which meant that I might get chewed up by his props. To avoid this at all costs, I decided to move over towards a grassy area on the left side of the runway. I was doing about 120 mph, and the end of the field with its cement barrier was approaching fast. I had to turn the glider 180° and somehow head it in the opposite direction without cracking up. I dove the glider as low as I could, and when the left wing skid touched the ground, I gave it more left aileron. I needed to increase the drag on the skid and push it farther into the ground. I then gave the glider left rudder, causing it to make a slow, skidding left turn. By the time we completed our turn we were going about 50 mph. We were lucky to be alive! If that maneuver hadn't been done exactly correct, we could have done a series of cartwheels down the field and never lived to tell about it. I noticed my copilot breathed a sigh of relief when the glider finally came to a stop.

"You weren't worried, were you?" I asked him.

"Not very," he replied.

I think he was lying.

❖   ❖   ❖

I had been assigned to night flying for the 29th Squadron. One night I noticed that my name was down on the roster to fly as copilot.

I called Lt. Hamilton to find out why I was copiloting this flight, instead of piloting.

He said, "Well, we know you were an instructor; this time you will be flying copilot with a man by the name of Anderson. He is a flight officer, but he could really use some help. I didn't think you would mind."

I told the lieutenant I would be happy to help.

We took off about 1900 hours, behind a DC-3 tow plane, and climbed to about 3,000 feet. At this point Flight Officer Anderson turned to me and asked, "Why can't I get above that tow plane? No matter what I do, I am lower than the tow plane."

I was surprised by his question, then suddenly realized what he meant. Without laughing or cracking a smile, I had to explain to him that the tow plane was not really above us, it was below us. He was trying to follow the reflection, instead of the actual plane. I explained to him that inside the cockpit of the CG-4A, the glass could cause an optical illusion. The tow plane splits into two images—one going up, the other down. A more experienced pilot would keep watching for the split and bring the images back together; or, he could tell where the tow plane was by the angle of the rope.

I told Anderson to cut loose from the tow plane and to prepare for a landing. He cut loose, then asked how he was doing. "Everything looks good." I said.

"Am I too high?" he asked.

"No, you are just right. Everything is still looking good."

We were on final approach, ready to land on the runway, when suddenly Anderson put the nose down. We were headed straight into the ground. I grabbed the controls, not knowing if I had enough time to pull out of the dive. I got control of the glider and averted going in headfirst, but it was close. I found out later that Anderson had washed out of primary flight training. He had no depth perception and became disoriented during night flying. He should have never been allowed to fly any type of aircraft, let alone one with me in it!

Chapter 9

A SUPPORTING ROLE

England to Normandy (and back again)

In the fall of 1943, we boarded the *Monarch of Bermuda* in Palermo, bound for Scotland. The ship left the pier near nightfall as a storm was brewing—not the best time to be on the open waters of the Mediterranean. Right time or not, there we were, bouncing, pitching and yawing about, many of us as sick as dogs. The waves grew so high that a destroyer following us spent half of its time underwater.

At the end of our voyage, we offloaded. We then boarded trains from Scotland to the towns of Grantham and Walkeringham, located in England. The British had built an airbase nearby, designed to meet our every need. It had Nissan huts housing twenty men apiece, with beautiful stoves in the center. The buildings were all new; in fact, everything on the base was new, including the runways. We had hot and cold running water, showers, an officers' club, dining room and mess hall. This would be our home for the foreseeable future.

Our Group Engineering offices were first rate; they had ample blackboards where we posted our status reports on every plane and glider. It was my job to maintain status reports on all 100 gliders. We had two sergeants assigned to the Engineering Group; one to inspect gliders, the other to inspect DC-3s. A man called "Skinny" Inman had been in the Group Engineering office for a couple of months and had achieved the rank of captain. He maintained status reports on all DC-3s.

Skinny was a rather odd fellow. He had been a pilot, but he had a series of unfortunate experiences that caused him to give up flying. He had spent many months recuperating in the hospital, trying to forget what had happened on the Salerno mission. He had told me he never wanted to get in an airplane again. I could never understand why, so I asked him to tell me the story.

He said, "Alright, I'll tell you. My orders were to fly a DC-3 loaded with paratroopers and drop them over Salerno. We got over the drop zone, and I gave the green light for the paratroopers to make the jump. All the paratroopers bailed out without incident. We were flying along at about 1,000 feet when I noticed an airplane about fifty feet above and just in front of me. I thought the plane was climbing out of the drop zone, after it had already dispatched its string of paratroopers.

But I watched in horror as the paratroopers started to bail out of the airplane just above me. The pilot kept going in the same direction and at the same elevation. He had no idea of what was about to happen. The paratroopers were coming down right in front of us, landing in our engines. They were pulverized like hamburger meat. The plane was full of blood; it was running down the fuselage and coming through the windows. These poor souls kept slamming into the props, and the props kept chewing them up until all twenty had died a gruesome death. While there was nothing we could have done to prevent this tragic accident, I felt, and still feel, somehow responsible for the tragedy. We went back to the field and landed. I was immediately taken to a hospital where I have spent the last year. I just can't get those ghastly images out of my mind. I was released from the hospital two months ago. Now you know why I never want to fly again!"

I told Skinny that it was not his fault. It was the responsibility of the pilot and co-pilot to make sure there were no other planes following at a lower altitude before giving the okay for the paratroopers to jump. There was nothing he could have done to avoid what happened.

❖   ❖   ❖

My mother sent me a letter saying that my brothers, Joe and Jim, were in London. It would be a perfect opportunity to see them again. Joe was a B-17 crew chief and turret gunner. Under General Patton, Jim was in charge of demolitions. If Patton wanted a bridge blown up, Jim was his man.

I called Jim from the Group Engineering office to tell him I would take a train down to meet him at his base. When I opened the door of his barracks, Jim hollered, "Attention!" The enlisted men came to attention when they saw an officer had entered their barracks. Jim got a big kick out of that; he doubled over laughing. After a few seconds, he said, "Oh, hey. It's my brother!"

When I realized the prank, I quickly said, "As you were, men."

Jim and I then took a streetcar into London, where we met Joe at the Rainbow Club. All three of us knew that we shouldn't go into an officers' club, since Jim was a PFC and Joe a staff sergeant. The British were very strict about their "no fraternization" policy between officers and enlisted men.

I figured, to hell with it. We're going in and I don't care what happens. They can throw us out if they don't like it.

We went in, and not wanting to be conspicuous, found a secluded table in the corner. We ordered a sumptuous turkey dinner, with everything you could think of including the dressing, potatoes and cranberry sauce. For dessert, we had pumpkin pie and plum pudding with white sauce, which reminded me of my Aunt Agnes' delicious plum pudding. As I recall, it took her days to make. Our meal was fantastic.

During dinner we discussed the war and some of the dangerous situations we had found ourselves in. While I considered both of their jobs more dangerous than mine, Jim thought a glider pilot was the most dangerous. Joe, on the other hand, thought that Jim had the most dangerous job because when he wasn't blowing up bridges he was getting shot at from the air and from the ground. Joe's job as a turret gun operator on a B-17 may have been the most dangerous, because he was taking fire from anti-aircraft guns, machine guns and ME-109s.

Joe said, "At least I don't have to worry about ground combat and taking direct fire on the battlefield."

Jim said, "Yes, sometimes I'm all alone in my foxhole."

Joe, who always kept his sense of humor said, "Well, if I see you I'll wave to you, OK?"

We left the Rainbow Club that evening happy for the time we had spent together. Alone in our thoughts, we knew it might be the last time we would ever see each other.

✻   ✻   ✻

As planned, Airborne units led the invasion of Normandy. On June 6, 1944, I flew in the second wave of the invasion, as a copilot in a DC-3. Our plane was flying paratroopers from the 82nd Airborne Division. We were to make our drop near Ste. Mere-Eglise. We took off from Grantham, flying over the White Cliffs of Dover. In other circumstances, they would have been a beautiful sight.

As we headed across the channel, I realized that it was full of ships of every type; battleships, destroyers, landing craft, troop transports and minesweepers to name a few. You could practically walk across the channel on them—they were that thick. I would later find out that this was the largest armada ever assembled, nearly 5,000 ships.

When we finally came to the drop zone over Ste. Mere-Eglise, the pilot asked me to give the green light for the paratroopers to jump. Having remembered Skinny's story of the ill-fated mission, I decided I was going to make damn sure we were clear of lower flying planes behind us. I told the pilot to make a 360° turn, and while doing so to check his side of the plane. I would likewise check mine.

I told him, "If there are no planes within 100 feet of us, I'll give the thumbs-up for the drop."

We completed our turn and everything looked good. I gave the word, and in less than one minute, the paratroopers were out of the plane and we were turning back towards the White Cliffs of Dover. They looked much more resplendent this time.

While French and American forces were liberating Paris, General Patton was heading for Nancy, in an area between the Moselle and Sarre Rivers. This became known as the Lorraine Campaign. General Patton requested the 313th Troop Carrier Group fly in ammunition to fight the Germans in a heavily fortified area known as the Moselle Line.

We arranged to have three DC-3s outfitted to hold ammunition. It was everywhere, covering the entire floor of the DC-3's cargo hold.

Tom Crouse was piloting one of the DC-3s, and I was flying copilot. With three planes in all, two other officers were leading the formation. We left Grantham and crossed the channel heading toward Paris. As we headed east, we could see a weather system building up just ahead of us. The next thing we knew, we were flying into a thick fogbank. Because of the poor visibility, we had to fly in tight formation. The nose of our ship was practically touching the rudder of the ship ahead.

We flew on in the dense fog for what seemed like an eternity when suddenly, without any warning, the pilot of the lead plane screamed, "Pull up! Pull up!"

Tom had a good reaction time and pulled up immediately. He put the plane in a climbing chandelle. We then realized why the lead pilot had called out the warning. Outside of the cockpit window, we saw huge monoliths looming just under our wings. In that instant, I wondered if we would ever clear them and live to tell about it. They looked to be the size of small houses, twenty-, thirty- and forty-foot boulders that just barely passed underneath our fuselage. We flew on in the fog for another ten minutes, holding our breath and praying. Finally, we broke out of it and were in clear skies. We looked around for the other

Author standing on the London Bridge

two DC-3s to pop out of the fog, but soon realized we were all alone. The other two planes had vanished. We never saw either plane or their crews again, and have to assume that they crashed into the rocks.

After that harrowing incident, we climbed well above the fog to 5,000 feet, and got back on course for Paris. Tom was not only a good pilot, but he was a good navigator as well. We were confident that we would find Paris, and General Patton would get his ammunition.

We had been flying along for quite some time when we noticed a DC-3 from another carrier group had joined up with us. On the interphone I asked him, "What the hell do you think you are doing out there?"

He replied, "We're lost and you fellows look like you know where you are going. So we thought we'd follow you."

"Then I guess we're both lost," I replied.

While we knew we were approaching Paris, the fog was so thick that everything was socked in. Suddenly, sticking up through the fog, I saw the tip of the Eiffel Tower. Tom radioed the other pilot that we were heading for Le Bourget airfield in Paris. He told him to land first and we would follow him in. We certainly didn't want to take any chances of being hit from behind while landing with an airplane full of ammunition!

The field at Le Bourget was wet and muddy. The brakes were of little use; the wheels only skidded along in the mud. I said, "Tom, you have to fishtail this thing; you do know how to fishtail, don't you?"

Tom looked at me quizzically. "What are you saying?

"I'll do it," I said.

I took the rudder and began pushing it left and right. I kept doing this until the tail end of the plane began to zigzag back and forth. This was a maneuver I learned when landing "tail draggers" under similar conditions. It slowed the plane down enough, and we stopped just short of the end of the runway, a few feet from the perimeter fence. The ammunition was unloaded and placed on a truck heading to General Patton and his next campaign.

Before leaving Paris, we decided to go out for a good meal at a local restaurant. We had cause to celebrate; Paris had been liberated by the French 2nd Armored Division under General Jacques-Philippe LeClerc. That division had been attached to Patton's 3rd Army. As for us, we had also completed our mission successfully.

We saw a sign for what looked to be a fancy place in the heart of Paris. It was located on the second floor of a beautiful building. We ordered champagne and a six-course dinner. The food was superb. The five of us were enjoying ourselves thoroughly until the bill arrived. They had charged us an outrageous amount for the champagne. When we protested, and said we were not going to pay so much, they grabbed our crew chief and took him to the kitchen, saying they would make him work it off. That's a fine how-do-you-do, I thought. The Americans had just liberated Paris and our point of view was given no consideration.

Tom told me to go downstairs and guard the main entrance of the restaurant. I pulled out my .45 and held my position at the foot of the stairs. Tom and the others drew their weapons and went to the kitchen to rescue our crew chief. We left the restaurant without further incident. At this point, we decided we had better head back to Le Bourget airfield and return to our base in Grantham.

We knew it would be prudent to stop for refueling rather than risk running out of gas on the way home, so we stopped at a British base where we put on 100 gallons of aviation fuel. We were shocked to see that the British had jacked up the price by about 400 percent—for fuel produced in the United States and given to England through the "lend lease" program. I was as mad as hell! Begrudgingly, I signed for the fuel and headed back to our base in Grantham.

❖   ❖   ❖

It was in mid-winter 1944 when I noticed a fellow coming around filling up the coal hod in each barracks. He was wearing a prisoners' armband. One day I stopped him, and asked what he was charged with.

"Insubordination," he replied.

"Who charged you?" I asked.

"Lieutenant Becker."

I said, "You need some help. You need someone to defend you, don't you?"

He said, "Yes, Sir."

I told him I would get him the best lawyer I could find. "Tell me all the details. What exactly put you in this situation?"

He said, "Right now I have to deliver coal . . . but I have a rest period coming up. I'll come back and tell you the whole story."

"Okay," I said, "don't forget now . . ."

"I won't. And thank you, Sir," he replied.

In about a half hour, he came back and we sat in the barracks while he recounted what had happened.

"I went into a bar. It was just another British pub serving commissioned and non-commissioned officers. It was kind of dark inside. There was a big shelf inside the front door where everyone placed their hats before getting a drink," he said.

"When I had finished drinking, I picked up my hat off the shelf, put it on and went outside. A few minutes later, Lt. Becker came out with his hat in his hand. He saw me in my hat and said, 'You have my hat on, son.'

"I said, 'I do?'

"'You do, and why aren't you standing at attention?'

"'I can't, Sir, I had too much to drink,' I replied.

"'Oh, is that how it is? Then I am going to charge you with insubordination. First you stole my hat, then you refused to stand at attention!'

"So, I gave Lieutenant Becker back his hat, and he immediately put it on. Lieutenant Becker then asked me, 'Is this your hat?'

"'Yes,' I said.

"'Well, you left your hat in the pub and picked up mine. You were impersonating an officer!'

"So, that's the story. Lieutenant Becker charged me with impersonating an officer and insubordination for wearing his hat and for not standing at attention."

I then asked the kind, slightly built man, who I now knew was PFC Smith, if he was being held in the brig when not delivering coal. He told me yes, he was.

He wore a prisoner's armband and was being treated as though he had already been convicted of the charges—even though he had yet to go to trial. I told PFC Smith I would find a lawyer to represent him.

I went over to see my chaplain, Captain James McArthur, and told him of the circumstances behind the charges PFC Smith was facing. After he listened to the story, I asked him if he thought he could help PFC Smith find good representation. He said, "I'm sure I can. But first I am going straight to command to report this incident." Since Captain McArthur was also a chaplain, he could bypass the normal channels and go directly to command.

On the day of Smith's court martial, I decided to confront Lt. Becker directly. I went over to his barracks and I told him that I needed to talk to him. "Let's go outside," I suggested.

I then asked him why the hell he was charging this kid with insubordination, when he and I both knew he was not guilty? I asked him if he remembered the time we were flying outside of Palermo in a DC-3 cargo plane. "We hit turbulence and began floating around the cabin of the DC-3. Your hat came off your head, my hat came off mine and we both were floating around the cabin. When the turbulence stopped, you ended up wearing my hat and I ended up wearing yours. You didn't charge me with insubordination. Did you?"

"No."

"Then why are you charging this kid? If you take the stand to testify against Smith, I will take the stand right after you to contradict every word you say."

I asked him if he remembered the time when we were at Camp Kilmore together, and he went AWOL in order to spend some time with his wife. "If you recall, you asked me to warn you if we ever went on alert while you were gone," I reminded him. "Well we did, and I went to the captain in charge of the Group and told him I needed to go get you. He told me that if I left the camp and was caught, he would not back me up. I would have been AWOL and in a lot of trouble, but I decided to leave camp anyway in order to warn you of the alert. When you came back to camp the next day, you were not punished, but promoted to lieutenant. Some of the other GI's who had gone off base were not so lucky. They were arrested and court martialed! That wasn't fair, now was it?"

I continued, "Then I will bring up the time you ordered flight officers to do manual labor, in violation of Air Force regulations."

Getting fed up, I finally said, "I don't get it; why do you have to court martial this kid?"

He replied, "I can't back down now. The adjutant wants me to make an example of him."

"Well," I said, "go ahead make an example out of him, but when I take the stand, I'll give the court another example, if you know what I mean."

I went back to Captain McArthur and told him of my conversation with Becker, and that if necessary, I would testify in PFC Smith's behalf.

The next day the trial began. Lt. Becker took the stand, and the defense attorney asked him to explain the incident leading up to the court martial.

Becker told the court, "PFC Smith failed to come to attention when ordered to do so, was insubordinate to me and is guilty of impersonating an officer."

The defense attorney asked him to explain how PFC Smith had impersonated an officer. "Well," he said, "he was wearing my hat at the time and thus was impersonating an officer."

"And why is PFC Smith guilty of insubordination?"

"Well," Becker said, "he was gyrating. He was gyrating all over the place."

The defense attorney asked, "I don't understand how people gyrate. I know what gyros[10] are. We have gyrocompasses and gyroscopes, and I know how a gyro works. But exactly how does a

---

[10] A navigational compass containing a gyroscope rotor, which when adjusted for the latitude and speed of the vessel or aircraft, indicates the direction of true north along the surface of the earth. (Source: Dictionary.com Unabridged [v1.1])

human being gyrate?" (this was before Elvis). Would you please demonstrate for the court?"

"I can't really show you . . .," replied Becker.

"Then just show us approximately how one gyrates."

Lt. Becker got up and started swaying his hips. The judge, while trying to suppress his laughter, said that the court was now in recess. He ordered that the proceedings reconvene the following morning at 0900.

That evening, I went over the details of the case with Chaplain Mc Arthur, and he said he had let Command know how the case was progressing. When we reconvened the following day, the first thing the judge did was to read a telegram he had received from command stating, "Release the prisoner."

The lawyer for the prosecution countered by telling the judge "new evidence had come to light," and that they would have it in their hands by tomorrow.

Chaplain James McArthur, at the Queen Victoria Memorial in front of Buckingham Palace

PFC Smith was again held in custody until the new evidence could be presented. The court martial was again adjourned until the following day.

The next morning, another telegram arrived from Command stating, "For a second time, release the prisoner." The judge sent a reply stating, "We are still gathering evidence that is vital to this case."

The following day another telegram arrived from the CO of the 313th Group stating, "For the third and last time, release the prisoner."

The judge finally called the proceedings to order and said, "The prisoner is to be released from custody."

All charges against Smith were dropped. He was released from custody, and Lt. Becker retained his rank. I am happy to say all ended well for both parties—and I can only imagine why the court martial was aborted so suddenly.

❖　　❖　　❖

When you want to go somewhere in England, and you ask someone if they know where that place is, you do not get an exact answer. In fact, you get sent on a very roundabout journey. For example, I wanted to know where Wednesbury was, so I asked one of the townspeople. "Oh yes," he said, "that's right outside of Sedgley."

"And where is Sedgley?"

"Sedgley is right outside of Salisbury."

"Where is Salisbury?"

"Salisbury is right outside of Manchester."

"Well, where is Manchester?"

"Manchester is just outside of London."

Under these circumstances, I managed to find my way around.

While I was in England, my father and aunt had asked me to try to find the graves of two of their siblings who had died in childhood. They told me they had been buried at a church in Sedgley. I went there in search of the parish priest, in hopes he would show me where the two graves were. One boy was named Alfonse, the other, William. They were buried in a little garden near the front of the church. Their graves were marked with only their names on the headstones. I sent a picture of the cemetery and graves to my dad and aunt.

Next, I went to see an old family friend by the name of Mr. Knight. He was the postmaster of Wednesbury. He had a daughter with the same name as my wife. During this time of war, she had been working on a farm. Mr. Knight introduced me to several families who said they had known my family. They showed me around town and pointed out the general store my grandfather, also named Mark Bagley, used to own. Another family invited me for afternoon tea and crumpets. That was a real treat.

The next stop was my great aunt's house. The first thing I saw when she opened the door was a large oil painting of my Uncle Joe. I said, "That's my Uncle Joe."

She almost keeled over. "How do you know Uncle Joe?"

133

I explained that when I was seven years old, he came to Massachusetts to visit. He had a brand new car. I was fascinated and couldn't keep my hands off it, touching everything, trying to figure out how it worked. He told me he was going to tie me to one of the wheels if I didn't stop fooling around!

My family had come to America from Wednesbury, England in search of their beloved son, John. John had gone to America in the 1890s. My grandparents never found him, but it was during that trip that they decided to bring their other children over. Thus, the Bagley family settled in Bedford, Massachusetts after leaving their home in England.

After strolling around the picturesque town of Wednesbury, we decided to take a bus to Coventry, a city Hitler had practically wiped off the face of the earth. There was nothing much to see but rubble and dust.

That evening I returned to Mr. Knight's house. He invited me to stay overnight and said that he would take me to the Minton[11] factory the next day to look around. The next morning we took a bus up to the town of Minton where the factory was located. I purchased six beautiful pieces of china to send home to Mary. I wanted to buy an entire set of china for her, but they did not have one available. They said they would continue that pattern after the war, if I wanted to buy more then.

I continued looking around the factory and noticed that they were using a vacuum pump to evacuate air and water from the clay. Their pump was not very efficient. I told them about a pump the Foxboro Company made that would do a much better job. You see, that is what makes chinaware so dense. You can have a very thin piece of bone china, yet it is remarkably strong.

One of the things that I learned was that after the china was fired the first time, the design was then hand painted using a product that was perfectly clear. The color showed up after the china was fired for a second time.

It was time to say goodbye to Mr. Knight and Wednesbury. I thanked him for his hospitality and asked if there was anything I

---

[11] In the 19th century, the Minton china factory was the most popular source of made-to-order dinnerware for embassies, heads of state and the like. In the 1820s, the Minton factory began to produce fine bone china, which is porcelain containing bone ash. Minton continues to uphold its reputation for organizational acumen and excellence in design, and is still in production today. (Source: www.thepotteries.org)

could get him to repay his kindness. "Oh," he said, "I would love a pound of cheese."

"OK," I said. "The next time I come to visit, I'll bring it to you."

The six pieces of Minton china were carefully packed for the trip home. I later carried them to London, through France and across the ocean to the United States. Not a single piece was broken. That was truly amazing and my wife was thrilled when she saw it. I only wish I could have brought her more.

❖   ❖   ❖

One morning I decided to take some leave time to search out the Foxboro-Yoxall Ltd. Company, the parent organization of the company I worked for back in Foxboro, Massachusetts. I took the train from Grantham down to London. I located the Foxboro-Yoxall Ltd. company quite easily. I wanted to meet Mr. Yoxall personally. I opened the front door of the office and the receptionist greeted me. I told her that I did not have an appointment, but that I wished to see Mr. Yoxall.

"Oh," she said, "he never sees anybody without an appointment."

"You tell him that I was an engineer for the Foxboro Company before the war, and worked at the home office in Foxboro, Massachusetts. I am sure he will be happy to meet with me," I said.

The receptionist disappeared for a little while and returned with Mr. Yoxall. We shook hands, and I introduced myself. I told Mr. Yoxall I was serving as a glider pilot in the 82nd Airborne; he seemed to be very impressed. I told him I would like to take a tour of his factory, if he could spare the time. He said he would be very pleased to show me around. We went through every department. The offices were similar to our facility in Foxboro; I explained that I was in charge of the training school working under Al Herschel. Part of my job was to teach students to calibrate Foxboro instrumentation.

"Do you have any such facility here?" I asked.

"Oh yes," he replied. "We have an excellent training school. We teach calibration for the various instruments we manufacture here."

Then Mr. Yoxall invited me to join him for lunch.

"We will finish our tour after our meal," he said.

We went to a wonderful restaurant. The food was superb, no doubt the best meal I had while in England.

After lunch we resumed our tour of the factory. Suddenly, we heard a number of buzz bombs overhead. Mr. Yoxall told me not to worry, that they were going right over our heads.

"How do you know?" I asked.

He said, "If you can hear the motor buzzing it is not going to hit you—it's when you can't hear it that you better run for cover."

As we listened intently to the incoming bombs, we realized that one of them had shut down.

"Quickly," Mr. Yoxall said, "let's get under these steel benches, this one is going to hit!"

I dove under one bench and he went under the other. The bomb landed next door, on top of a greenhouse. It made one hell of a noise when it exploded and everything shook violently. After the explosion, we got to our feet and looked out of the shattered factory windows into a gaping hole in the ground. The greenhouse had completely disappeared.

At this point, I decided it was a good time to say goodbye to Mr. Yoxall and thank him for his time and hospitality. I asked if there was anything I could get for him at the PX.

"I would love five pounds of cheese. I have not had any since the war began," he said.

I told him, "The next time I go on leave, I promise to bring you some. If I can't make it back here, I will mail it to you. Either way, you will get your cheese." We shook hands and I left.

I then went on a mission to find a modestly priced hotel room in London for the night, somewhere I could get a warm bath. After searching the city, I finally found a room with an old-fashioned bathtub and an added bonus—hot running water! I drew an extra-hot bath and climbed in. The tub was one of those heavy cast iron monstrosities with gaudy claw feet. I must have been soaking for about ten minutes when I heard another buzz bomb flying overhead.

I thought to myself, oh hell, I might as well stay right here. I have a heavy iron shell around me, so I should be safe from any exploding bomb fragments. I just stayed right there in the tub relaxing as it flew past.

Once my skin was sufficiently shriveled, I got out of the tub. By then the attack had stopped and I drifted into a deep sleep. The next morning I awoke feeling refreshed. I caught the train in London and headed back to my base in Grantham.

A few days later, I went down to the PX and bought two boxes of cheese, one for Mr. Knight and one for Mr. Yoxall. I mailed them just as I promised. I hope both men enjoyed their small token of my appreciation. Unfortunately, I never saw either of them again.

Waco CG-4A at the National Museum of the United States Air Force
(U.S. Air Force photo)

Chapter 10

IN THE THICK OF IT

Operation Market-Garden

Early in September, Major Andross, the 313th Group Glider Operations Officer, held a briefing for all Group glider pilots on Operation Market-Garden.

He said, "General Montgomery has convinced General Eisenhower of his plan to use the entire newly-formed First Allied Airborne Army, consisting of three and one-half divisions, for a mass attack into Holland."

This gigantic Airborne force was to seize a series of bridges in Holland, between Eindhoven and Arnhem, beginning with the southern-most bridge over the Meuse-Escant Canal. Next was to be the Zon Bridge over the Wilhelmina Canal, then additional canal bridges at St. Oedenrode and Veghal. Heading north, the next key bridge was at Grave over the huge Maas River, followed by the Nijmegen Bridge over the Waal River. The most northern and last bridge was at Arnhem, over the lower Rhine river.

The 313th Troop Carrier gliders were to land the 82nd Airborne infantry troops in the area of Nijmegen, between the Waal and Maas Rivers. The first wave was scheduled for takeoff on 17 September. The second wave was to follow the next day.

On September 20, General Montgomery's tanks of the British Second Army were scheduled to race through the Northbound Corridor from Eindhoven, Nijmegen and Arnhem. They were to cross the lower Rhine River, sweep through the Rurh and roll up the German lines all the way to Berlin.

The code name for this operation was "Market-Garden." "Market," covering the airborne paratroops, drop zones, gliders and landing zones; "Garden," covering the armored divisions. The First Allied Airborne Army consisted of a 35,000 man force; to transport this force into Belgium almost 600 air miles away required over 1,500 gliders. We had an excess of available gliders, but were short on C-47 Dakotas and Dakota pilots for a single-wave operation, hence the two-wave operation planned for September 17 and 18, 1944.

I remember listening in disbelief as Major Andross said, "Each glider of the 313th Troop Carrier Group will be flown by a single crew member. Pilot only, no copilot. In this manner, our group can fly in 200 gliders, instead of the customary 100. And, by the way, there are an insufficient number of parachutes in the European theatre of operation to provide parachutes for all airborne personnel in compliance with U.S. Army Air Force regulations. Glider pilots are hereby ordered to leave their assigned parachutes in the storage tent. No on-board glider personnel are to be provided with parachutes. Glider pilots will be provided with bulletproof vests for flak protection.

"Once we cross the English Channel, we will fly along the Holland coast before turning inland on a southeast-by-east heading for Arnhem. The tow plane pilots have been briefed on flying a specific route, through narrow airspace corridors. We are to be escorted to our landing zones by 1,500 planes, including P-47s, Thunderbolts, P-51 Mustangs, Mosquitoes and Spitfires. We will protect and escort the Airborne troops of the First Allied Airborne Army to their destinations."

Again, he reminded us that all Dakota pilots were instructed to fly in an in-line train formation through the narrow designated corridors for maximum safety.

As Major Andross had said, a massive single-wave operation was considered for Market-Garden, which required 2,929 Dakotas and 1,954 gliders, for a total of 4,883 Airborne aircraft. The 9th Troop Carrier Command was short by more than 700 Dakotas and crews; hence this concept was not feasible, and consequently never implemented.

Instead, a two-day, two-wave mission was scheduled for September 17, 1944, involving 2,953 aircraft, and for September 18, involving 1,530 aircraft.

Major Andross' briefing incited a lot of concern and questions from glider pilots, engineers and operations officers. For one, we were being ordered to fly troop-carrying aircraft deep behind enemy lines with no co-pilot. And two, we were being ordered to fly troop-carrying aircraft behind the lines without parachutes for pilot or passengers!

First, U.S. Army Air Force Regulations required that all dual control transports, bombers and gliders be manned by both pilot and co-pilot. Secondly, U.S. AAF Regulation 002A stipulated that *all* personnel on board *any* U.S. AAF aircraft must be provided with a parachute.

In discussion with the other glider pilots, I pointed out that not all personnel on board U.S. AAF bombers and Dakota transports were provided with parachutes. Although the B-17 Crew Chief, Tail Gunner and Belly Gunner were issued parachutes, they could not wear them because of cramped quarters. Additionally, a general could order someone to fly without a parachute, but it is not a court martial offense if they refuse. I recalled that in Sicily, I had refused an order to lead a fifteen-glider flight because parachutes were not provided by Operations. I held up the takeoff until parachutes were provided in accordance with regulations. But for this operation, questions remained in my mind. Were those in command justified in issuing such orders?

Continuing our "meeting," we glider pilots questioned if safe parachute deployment could be attained from a 400-foot altitude. We all agreed it would not be safe to attempt a free fall without static lines to open the chute. At 140 mph, could we gain an additional 600 feet to make a safe jump at 1,000 feet? The answer came back a resounding "No!"

We glidermen agreed that although "by the book" our orders were not valid, Air Force regulations did not provide for the conditions encountered. Parachutes had saved the lives of many glider pilots, when their gliders came apart in midair, or began a series of outside loops for no apparent reason. Then one of us asked, "Even if we were provided with parachutes but lost a wing, do you think the 82nd Airborne would allow us to bail out?" Hell no, they would expect us to do our very best to land the troops safely. So, the glider pilots of the 313th made a decision. We would fly the mission without parachutes.

The next item of controversy was the order eliminating our co-pilots. Up to this point in the war, all troop-carrying gliders and Dakotas had been provided with pilot and co-pilot for maximum reliability and safety. When an aircraft is piloted by a single pilot, and that pilot is killed, the crew members and passengers will likely be killed as well. In our situation, Dakota transports would be towing our gliders into their landing zones at an altitude of 400 feet where they would face fire from enemy aircraft, small-arms fire, machine gun fire, anti-aircraft fire and rifle fire. Our conclusion? This single pilot, parachute-less operation would be damned risky!

There is an enormous amount of managing on the part of engineering officers, crew chiefs and maintenance personnel for every airborne mission. Each glider must be inspected to ensure that all technical orders from Washington are followed, and to certify the glider is air-worthy. Drag chutes, used for deceleration on rapid letdowns, must be operational on all gliders. These are but a couple of the Squadron Glider Engineering Officer's responsibilities. As Group Glider Engineering Officer, I had four squadrons of CG-4As to make ready.

About ten percent of our gliders had a Griswold[12] nose section, designed to cut steel cables that might be encountered during landing. Factory installed radios were in all gliders, but they were battery-powered and required regular operational check-ups. The radio pack was designed as a snap-out walkie-talkie, which was to be used for ground communications after landing. Glider towlines had telephone cables to enable tow plane-to-glider communication. Of course, during the actual mission, absolute radio silence was crucial.

Glider pilots had their choice of weapons. I chose a .45-caliber grease gun with seven slips of thirty cartridges each. I also got a .45-caliber sidearm with four clips of six cartridges each, and several packs of .45-caliber shells of one hundred cartridges each. My theory was, one size cartridge for both guns, hence no fumbling with mixed guns and shells; reloading would be simple, especially in close combat. And rapid firing would be essential. In addition, I chose three hand grenades, a combat knife, boots, jacket, maps, compass, K-rations, gas mask and tent. The total weight was over 100 pounds. We were told not to take our gas equipment into combat, but I chose to take mine anyway. Our bulletproof vest weighed over forty pounds and felt like a radiation shield at a dentist's office.

I installed sandbags in the nose section of the glider, under the pilot and co-pilot's seats. On top of the seat, I placed a 14-inch square, steel armor plate, three-quarters of an inch thick for added protection.

---

[12] This device was developed to combat the Germans' use of steel cables across our landing zones. Placed at approximately five feet above the ground, the cables would decapitate glider passengers and crew. The Griswold nose section used steel guide channels attached to the glider's Plexiglas nose, which caused the cables instead to slip over the top of the glider. It also included a steel cutting blade, placed at the peak of the nose section, designed to cut through the cables.

The weather was clearing; stratus clouds provided forty percent sky cover, with a deep blue background and a light westerly wind. This was Sunday morning, September 17, 1944. The first wave of troop-carrying planes, gliders and their tow planes took off from airfields all over England for their four-hour flight to Holland. Operation Market-Garden had begun.

There were 2,953 troop carrier aircraft (1,089 of which were gliders) with 23,000 troops, 336 vehicles, 220 artillery pieces and 400 tons of cargo all aloft, circling in holding patterns from twenty-odd air bases, awaiting their turn to cross the English channel. Two, 300-mile long trails were established, one for gliders and the other for troop carriers.

I was scheduled to depart England with the second wave, scheduled for Monday, September 18. The second-wave gliders were all air-worthy and ready for takeoff. My responsibilities were complete, and that allowed me time to observe the first wave takeoffs. I was amazed at the skills of both tow plane pilots and glider pilots working in harmony. It was a vast improvement since the days of Casablanca and Sicily over one year earlier; now our pilots were experienced. For example, I observed that whenever the tow plane lifted off the runway, the pilot did not immediately retract his landing gear. He knew that if the glider was not yet airborne, he would be right back on the runway due to the added drag caused by the glider lifting off. Most of these gliders were heavily loaded and required greater than normal speed before liftoff. Some gliders lifted off before their tow planes and some tow planes lifted off before their gliders. However, they all knew how to compensate to maximize lift and minimize drag.

The next morning, the second wave lined up on the runway with engines and pilots ready for takeoff. After waiting more than three hours for clearance, the mission was called off due to inclement weather at the landing zones. We went through the same procedure for an additional four days, and each day the mission was called off due to weather conditions in drop or landing zones. Finally, on Saturday, September 23, 1944, the second wave lifted off from various airfields in England, bound for drop and landing zones in Holland.

The Commanding Officer of the 49th Squadron was leading the four squadrons of the 313th Troop Carrier Group. I was second in the formation, being towed by my buddy Lt. Tom Crause. The next in formation was Major Stovall, with his glider in tow.

Tom called and advised we would be in our holding area in twenty minutes. We would continue to circle until instructed to move out toward the channel.

I had fourteen Airborne infantrymen on board. Their second lieutenant was sitting in the co-pilot's seat. I asked him if he ever had any flying instruction. His answer was "No." It is impossible to try to teach flying when the glider is in a constant turn, but I tried anyway. No luck; he was not able to keep it in the turn. I told him, "If I'm shot just get me off the controls and cut loose. Don't try to fly the glider, stay away from the controls." In case the unthinkable happened, I had the trim tabs set to establish a shallow glide, so the glider would stabilize itself and prevent a high-speed nosedive.

The crewmember sitting directly behind me kept asking, "Lieutenant, do you want a piece of candy?" I kept saying no. I don't remember how many times he asked, but he must have had a hundred of them.

After three and a half hours of circling, we were given clearance to proceed on a heading to our destination. Tom and I had a direct telephone line, which we kept open at all times during the tow. The sky was now nearly covered with altostratus clouds; visibility was unlimited, and we were just passing over the White Cliffs of Dover heading seaward.

I suddenly remembered a song and wondered if I would ever see my wife again. The lyrics went:

"Put on your old grey bonnet with the blue ribbon on it / And I'll hitch old Dobbin to the shay

We will ride into Dover / Through the fields of clover / On our Golden Wedding Day." ("Golden Wedding Day," by Stanley Murphy and Percy Wenrich)

After crossing the channel, we let down to 400 feet on a northeast heading for Holland. We were flying over a beautiful green forest. The breeze was a zero on the Beaufort[13] scale; not a leaf was turning or moving. The forest looked calm and inviting.

About a mile off our port side streamed a trail of several hundred Dakotas approaching at a 15° angle. We were cruising at 140 mph, and they were cruising at 125 mph. I estimated that they would intercept our flight path in about ten minutes, at a point about six miles ahead. In a few minutes, I could visualize the point of

---

[13] A scale and description of wind velocity ranging from calm (0) to hurricane (12).

interception, which happened to be over a small hill. As their lead plane approached the hill, I observed ominous gray and black puffs of flak from German antiaircraft fire. The paratroops' lead plane immediately veered to the left, and thus the balance of the formation avoided the deadly flak area.

Wondering about our CO, I asked Tom, "What do you think? Is the old man going to change course, or what?"

"I don't know," Tom replied. "We can't break radio silence and we have to remain with the formation."

"Tom, we will be over the flak in three minutes. We're sunk!"

We didn't have to wait long; as soon as the CO's plane came into the flak area, all hell broke loose. He was in the lead on my port side; suddenly, his plane burst into a fireball, then his glider cut loose and was going down. The plane hurtled nose down at 100 feet, heading towards an uncontrolled crash. On my starboard side, Major Stovall's Dakota was also on fire; his glider cut loose and was going down for a crash landing. The antiaircraft guns kept pounding away, but that was not their only weapon. They threw all kinds of small arms fire in our direction—machine guns, pistols, rocket launchers, rifles and rifle grenades. When I looked down, I saw nothing but sparks and flashes emanating from all those firing guns. Tracers seemed to quickly rise and pass silently through the fabric covering of my glider. I tried to make myself as small as possible, to fit over the steel plate under my seat. Suddenly, there was silence once again; we had passed over the hot spot. Amazingly, everyone on board was fine; there were no injuries. To calm my nerves, I asked the soldier sitting behind me if I could now have a piece of candy. He replied, "Sorry, Sir; they're all gone. . ."

Tom was on the interphone asking how everything was with us. I advised him that all was OK and that no one had gotten hurt. I asked him if his crew was all right. Surprisingly, Tom replied, "No problems; no injuries here either." Then he said, "I want you to look me over, top to bottom, and see if there are any holes or leaks." I climbed up to fifty feet above the tow and found no problems. I then went into the low-tow position and examined the bottom of the plane.

I told Tom, "No problems, except your co-pilot's wheel is going down slowly. Looks like your hydraulic system may be damaged. You can always operate the gear manually, so you should be OK."

"Thanks!" Tom replied, with relief in his voice.

I knew we were getting close to our landing zone when I spotted a river on the horizon. At an altitude of 400 feet, the horizon is not far away. In a few minutes, we passed over the Maas River, and dead ahead I could make out the Waal River. We were to set down between these two rivers in the Nijmegen area. Tom called on the interphone and confirmed my thoughts. I was to pick the landing field of my choice.

I chose the field used by the 82nd Airborne Division for an earlier drop, which was almost covered with parachutes. I felt it would offer us adequate protection from German guns. If there were Airborne troops nearby, they could give us cover during unloading.

My final approach would be over a row of eighty-foot trees, spaced on twenty-foot centers. "Give me an additional 600 feet of altitude and I'll cut off at 1,000 feet," I said.

"Roger," Tom replied.

"Tom," I said, "seeing those hundreds of parachutes all in one field reminded me of what Mendez[14] had to say to troop carrier pilots." (Mendez had said, "When I brought my battalion to the briefing prior to Normandy, I had the finest force of its size that will ever be known. By the time I attempted to gather them together in Normandy, half were gone!")

So, I challenged Tom, "Put us down in Holland or put us down in Hell, but put us down together!" Looking at the ground below, I said, "From here, Tom, it looks like they were all put down together. Hey, what are you doing?"

Tom replied, "Got the side window open, snappin' a few pictures. Then after you cut off, I'm gonna look for a German jeep to drop the rope on . . . I call it ropin' the jeep."

Laughing, I thanked Tom for the tow and cut off; he waved his wings and zoomed away.

I quickly outlined my landing plan to a lieutenant who moved up next to me in the co-pilot's seat—I could use his help. "Our approach will be over the trees, in order to land into the wind. We are now approximately 600 feet from the trees, which we need to pass over. I'm going to open our drag chutes, and nose the glider down at a 45° angle. When we reach an altitude of 600 feet, we'll release the chute. That's your job, Lieutenant. Pull this ring when I tell you. We should clear the tree tops by 200 feet and make a soft landing."

---

[14] Lt. Col. Louis G. Mendez, Battalion Commander of the 82nd's 508th Regiment

I then opened the drag chute and nosed down. The airspeed went up to 135 mph and the altimeter was unwinding. We were at an altitude of 600 feet, so I shouted, "Release the drag chute!" The lieutenant looked at me with terror in his eyes and yelled, "It won't release!"

I quickly undid my seatbelt, stood up and pulled with all my might. Several anxious seconds seemed to pass like hours. In the back of my mind, I was thinking the worst. Suddenly, the ring and cable came out in my hand—the chute had finally released.

But we were now at an altitude of 150 feet, with absolutely no chance of clearing the trees just ahead. Then I remembered a story about a WWI pilot who made a crash landing between two trees somewhere in France in 1918. He hit the trees close to ground level. His wings came off and the fuselage shuddered to a stop a few feet farther on, but there were no injuries.

That was my plan now. With twenty feet between trees, there would be plenty of space for the fuselage to clear the trunks. I had checked my airspeed about 200 feet from the ground; it was 120 mph. I thought, why hit the trees if we can jump them? I pulled the control column straight back. The ship started to climb, but it was too late. We hit four trees simultaneously. Strangely, there was no sense of a bump, because we hit them at sixty feet up. We flew right through the trees without feeling or hearing a thing. I felt the left wing go down; I applied full right aileron, but the glider did not respond. We were about fifty feet above ground, at level flight but dropping fast. When we hit the ground, both wheels shot off and we skidded for about 100 feet. The fuselage was all in one piece, and by some miracle, there were no injuries to any of the troops.

For some reason, they all left the glider in a big hurry! I removed my heavy flak suit, put on my battle jacket, picked up my guns and ammunition, knapsack, map, compass and three hand grenades. I left the walkie-talkie, transmitter and first aid kit behind.

As I stepped out the glider door, I looked back at the four trees. Three of them were snapped off around the sixty-foot level. The fourth tree held the port side wing. I was surprised that the glider flew so well after losing it.

After this harrowing experience, I was beat, but decided to follow the 82nd Airborne troops. They were marching in a single column. As we left the landing area, I saw a large windmill located on a small hill. We were following a country road, with stone walls along each side.

We came to the banks of the river Maas, and turned in a northwest by westerly heading towards the great Maas Bridge.

I saw a road sign inscribed with the name "Groesbeek," with an arrow pointing eastward. We were heading west, but I made sure the name of the town was in my memory—just in case I had to look it up on my map later. We came to an intersection and headed south.

There was a bridge just ahead—it looked like the Cottage Farm Bridge that spans the Charles River between Boston and Cambridge. Heavy artillery fire or bombs had damaged its concrete flooring. Some of the holes measured between three and four feet in diameter. When I was about halfway across the bridge, I heard a hell of a lot of noise. It was being produced by a single P-51; he was about three feet above the water, heading toward the bridge at 300 mph. He flew under the bridge, then pulled up into an Immelman turn and disappeared. Except for the Dakotas, the P-51 was the only airplane I'd seen since leaving England.

After crossing the Maas, we came into the town of Grave. The streets were lined with women and children offering us apples, pears and lump sugar. They were so happy to see us. The infantry column halted and the troops took a half-hour rest period. I went over to a stone wall, found a comfortable spot and took a nap.

When I awoke, the infantry was gone. It was getting dark and I was all alone forty miles behind the lines, with nowhere to go. I needed to find a warm and comfortable place. Walking along the roadside, I eventually came to a nice looking barn. I opened the front door; the barn was used for storing hay for fodder. My uncle had such a barn in Bedford, Massachusetts, where as a kid I used to tumble and play. I fluffed up a soft bed of hay and went back to sleep.

Suddenly, I awoke to see the barn door opening very slowly. I could see two men, and recognized by their battle jackets and equipment that they too were glider pilots. But to be sure, I called out, "Who goes there?" They responded, "Glider pilots!" I welcomed them in and told them to make themselves at home. Additional glider pilots continued to drift in, one by one. By midnight, a dozen or more had arrived at our shelter. We were all relaxed and resting quietly, when all hell broke loose!

The night sky illuminated with flashes from massive guns on both sides. The sound of exploding shells sounded like the finale of a Fourth of July fireworks display. There were two lines of fire, one to the east about 4,000 feet and the other about the same distance to the west. We were caught in the crossfire.

OPERATION MARKET GARDEN
STATISTICAL INFORMATION

Gliders' Contribution to Operation Market Garden

Resource Flown In	British Horsa	American CG-4A
Troops	61	272
Artillery	75	145
Vehicles	112	224
Cargo	65	135

First Wave = 1,089 Gliders

Resource Flown In	British Horsa	American CG-4A
Troops	32	149
Artillery	35	75
Vehicles	58	116
Cargo	35	65

Second Wave = 565 Gliders

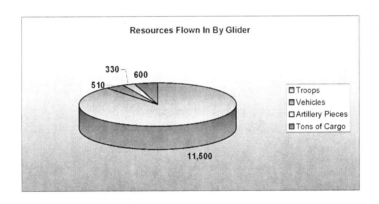

149

OPERATION MARKET GARDEN
STATISTICAL INFORMATION

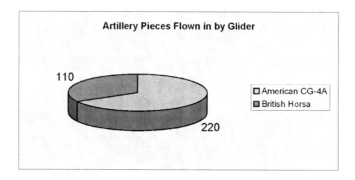

First Wave - Sunday, September 17, 1944	
British Horsa	**American CG-4A**
Gliders flew in 75 artillery pieces + 4 troops per piece	Gliders flew in 145 artillery pieces + 4 troops per piece

Second Wave - Sunday, September 23, 1944	
British Horsa	**American CG-4A**
Gliders flew in 35 artillery pieces + 4 troops per piece	Gliders flew in 75 artillery pieces + 4 troops per piece

	British Horsa	American CG-4A
Sunday, September 17, 1944	130 tons	270 tons
Saturday, September 23, 1944	70 tons	130 tons
	Cargo Gliders Flew in 600 Tons Total	

OPERATION MARKET GARDEN
STATISTICAL INFORMATION

Number of C-47 Dakota Transports Required

First Wave - September 17, 1944

For Paratroopers	775
Tow Planes for Horsa Troop Gliders	61
Tow Planes for Horsa Vehicle Gliders	112
Tow Planes for Horsa Artillery Gliders	75
Tow Planes for Horsa Cargo Gliders	65
Tow Planes for CG-4A Troop Gliders	272
Tow Planes for CG-4A Vehicle Gliders	224
Tow Planes for CG-4A Artillery Gliders	145
Tow Planes for CG-4A Cargo Gliders	135
Total C-47 Dakota Air Transports	**1,864**

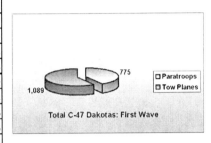

Total C-47 Dakotas: First Wave

Second Wave - September 23, 1944

For Paratroopers	400
Tow Planes for Horsa Troop Gliders	32
Tow Planes for Horsa Vehicle Gliders	58
Tow Planes for Horsa Artillery Gliders	35
Tow Planes for Horsa Cargo Gliders	35
Tow Planes for CG-4A Troop Gliders	149
Tow Planes for CG-4A Vehicle Gliders	116
Tow Planes for CG-4A Artillery Gliders	75
Tow Planes for CG-4A Cargo Gliders	65
Total C-47 Dakota Air Transports	**965**

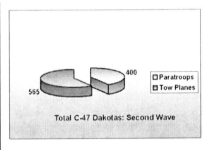

Total C-47 Dakotas: Second Wave

775 Paratroops
1,089 Tow Planes

400 Paratroops
565 Tow Planes

151

OPERATION MARKET GARDEN
STATISTICAL INFORMATION

	Resource	Glider Troops	Paratroops	Horsas	CG-4As	C-47 Dakotas
		First Wave Troop Carrier Command Aircraft				
	Troops		15,500			775
	Troops	1,752		61		61
	Troops	3,524			272	272
112	Vehicles	448		112		112
224	Vehicles	896			224	224
75	Artillery	300		75		75
145	Artillery	580			145	145
130	Tons Cargo			65		65
270	Tons Cargo				135	135
	Totals	7,500	15,500	313	776	1,864

23,000 Troops

1,089 Gliders

2,953 Total First Wave Troop Carrier Aircraft

	Resource	Glider Troops	Paratroops	Horsas	CG-4As	C-47 Dakotas
		Second Wave Troop Carrier Command Aircraft				
	Troops		8,000			400
	Troops	928		32		32
	Troops	1,936			149	149
58	Vehicles	232		58		58
116	Vehicles	464			116	116
35	Artillery	140		35		35
75	Artillery	300			75	75
70	Tons Cargo			35		35
130	Tons Cargo				65	65
	Totals	4,000	8,000	160	405	965

12,000 Troops

565 Gliders

1,530 Total Second Wave Troop Carrier Aircraft

To combine both the first and second wave operations into a massive single-strike operation required a total of 2,829 C-47 Dakotas and 1,654 gliders, for a total of 4,483 troop carrier aircraft. This plan was not feasible, however, due to a shortage of several hundred Dakotas and their crews.

Our supposed refuge was at the apex of their mortar, rocket and shelling trajectory. The sounds of rifles and bazookas intermingled. We could not differentiate the firing patterns between the two sides. I was unfamiliar with the sounds generated by any of them; so were the other pilots. In spite of the shelling, we all went back inside to decide what our course of action would be. It was unanimous; the defense of the barn would be simple. We all positioned ourselves in the center. If the enemy came through one door, we would open fire and exit through the opposite door.

At long last, the shelling eased and all became silent. Thank God for that; we could all get some much-needed rest.

The crowing of a rooster just outside awakened me. It was Sunday, and church bells began to chime. In stark contrast to the turmoil and darkness of the night before, it was sunny and warm; couples were walking to church on this peaceful morning.

We decided to contact someone from the village that could advise us and offer directions. We knocked on the farmhouse door, a short distance from the barn. A man came to the door, but he did not speak English. We showed him our map, tracing our fingers along our intended route. He shook his finger and said, "No! No! . . .Cherman!" We traced an alternate route a little farther to the east. He said, "Oh, no . . . CHERMANS!" One of the pilots asked the question, "Should we trust him?" I said, "We have no choice."

If we had learned one thing from our contact with the Germans, it was a tactic to help us stay alive behind German lines. I reminded everyone, "We have to file out of here in single file, at five-minute intervals. The German snipers will not give away their firing position to kill a single man."

So, we drew straws. I was number seven. After each man left our area, the rest of us would listen, trying to detect gunshots. My turn approached and so far, no shots; I felt relatively safe and started out on our selected route. I walked in silence for a half mile, when an 82nd paratrooper jumped out of some roadside bushes and shouted, "Halt and identify!" I answered, "Glider pilot; my orders are to report to your command post." He advised me that the command post was around the next bend, on the left side, uphill about 1,000 feet. I then noticed two or three antitank guns all seemed to be pointed at me. Other troops were all around, but they were so well camouflaged that they blended into the landscape.

The command post was in a tent-like structure in a small field, with a 360° view of the surrounding area. After reporting to the officer in charge, he told me, "We have no immediate need for you here. You are free to return to England." I asked if he had any suggestions on how I should proceed. He told me of an airport about a mile or so to the northwest, which he said might be worth looking into.

I went outside and looked to the northwest. I saw a Dakota on its takeoff run at a very low altitude, probably fifty feet. As it gained altitude, at approximately 600 feet, it came down in a ball of fire, which turned to heavy black smoke after impact. I decided that the airport was out of the question and headed for the main road south to Eindhoven.

I did not know it at the time, but I was going down Hell's Highway. This roadway, heading south out of Nijmegen, was a secondary single lane highway, like a narrow causeway. There were mature trees evenly spaced on both sides, and much of the road went along the tops of dikes.

I came upon a sandy section of roadway, with small trees and bushes along one side. Suddenly, two men came out of the bush, one of them carrying a white surrender flag. As they approached, I recognized them as German infantry. They were unarmed. I motioned for them to head south, and I followed about twenty feet behind. My machine gun was armed and ready for any surprises. As we passed by a bush, two 82nd paratroopers appeared as if by magic. I ordered them to take the two prisoners to the command center for interrogation. They saluted, and took them off my hands. I came to a bend in the roadway; the paratroopers and their prisoners were out of sight. Then I heard two very loud shots. I was shocked, and thought, Oh shit! Those bastards shot them!" I struggled with the feeling that it was all my fault.

I thought back to June, when I was at the 82nd Airborne's lockdown camp near Grantham, England. Chaplain McArthur and I went to visit with the troops prior to their D-Day jump. They told me that the 82nd paratroopers were known as the Red Devils, and would take no prisoners. I might have agreed with that point of view when in battle; but it should not apply if the enemy soldier is unarmed.

I walked for another hour or so until I heard a truck approaching from the north. It was a standard ten-wheel U.S. Army truck with benches on either side. The driver came alongside and asked if I wanted a ride. He was a young, very thin black man, all alone and unarmed. He was happy to have me aboard, especially with my stash of weapons. I got in the cab and we headed south. About every three or four miles, we overtook another glider pilot, who piled into the bench area behind the cab. We had collected ten glider pilots in about twenty miles of travel, and were soon approaching the Zon Bridge. The roadway was narrow and lined by large trees. Just ahead, we saw two tanks blocking our side of the road. One tank was attempting to pass the other. My compatriot at the wheel kept blowing his horn and headed toward the tank on our side. The truck was peeling bark off trees on my side as we passed. The tank got back in line, just as we sped by.

We were entering the thick of battle. Shells were coming in from the west; we could see trucks with infantrymen on board bursting into flames. They were then callously pushed off the highway by the tanks, trying to keep the highway open. The Germans were using an antiaircraft gun in the horizontal position. As the German guns opened fire, I saw three British tanks drive off the highway, knocking down trees and firing as they headed into a gun emplacement.

For miles, we passed dead British soldiers on each side of the highway. It was a horrifying sight. The noise from the shelling sounded like thunder, and the clanking from the tanks must have been close to ninety decibels. The Germans did not fire at our truck, because it was no threat; they were hitting armed vehicles. If we had stopped for any reason, the British tanks would have pushed our truck off the causeway too! It seemed as though we passed hundreds of British soldiers before coming to a complete stop at the Zon Bridge.

The Germans had three guns zeroed in on the bridge. Whenever they noticed troop movement, one of their guns would fire. Meanwhile, the British Army field engineers were constructing a Bailey[15] bridge; at that moment, it was almost complete.

Our truck had stopped alongside a British tank. The gun crew was out behind the tank, having a tea break. I told my fellow soldier that I wanted to talk with the Tank Commander, and would be right back. I asked the Commander why the Montgomery 2nd Army was five days late in their arrival. He said, "Weather." I told him I understood how the weather could affect aircraft, but asked how it could affect land troops. He replied, "It's been raining all week. Our tanks get bogged

---

[15] A prefabricated, sectional and portable steel bridge, which utilized quick connect and disconnect attachments for rapid field construction. It was used to replace blown bridges or to construct new bridges over rivers and streams. They were usually single-lane, but strong enough for tanks, vehicles or troops.

down in the mud and we have to stop and change our treads too often."

I got back on board the truck. The Bailey bridge was completed and they signaled us to come over first. In a few minutes, we were over the bridge and on our way to Eindhoven. As soon as the 2nd Army started to move northward, the Germans began shelling the bridge again. Several tanks from that division on each side of the Zon Bridge went speeding off the roadway, heading westward into the blazing German guns. A dozen or so vehicles made the crossing via the Bailey bridge before it was demolished.

Needless to say, progress was extremely slow and dangerous for the 2nd Army trying to reach Arnhem. I decided it was time to check up on our present position on Hell's Highway, and to determine if we had sufficient fuel to reach Brussels. We had another five or six miles to Eindhoven, to our front lines. Our fuel supply was adequate for us to reach Brussels safely, which was a distance of seventy miles.

This section of the roadway was littered with remains of an earlier battle, some of which was still smoking. Vehicles from the British 2nd Army continued to pass us on their way to Arnhem, which slowed our pace due to the narrow roadway and tight passing conditions.

Then the roadway suddenly changed to a standard highway. We had arrived at the outskirts of Eindhoven. We came to an intercrossing, at the center of which was a smoldering, burned-out German antiaircraft gun. We saw a sign at one of the intersections that said "Brussels," with an arrow indicating its direction. We were on our way. Before leaving the city limits, we came to a section with women on both sides of the street, trying to get our attention. I had the driver slow down to find out what it was all about. They were passing out handfuls of sugar cubes. The glider pilots in the back of the truck filled their pockets. I accepted several handfuls. The only reason we had for accepting the sugar was that it was such a heartfelt gift.

We had driven several miles after entering the outskirts of Brussels when I spotted a trolley car. I asked the truck driver to stop and pull over. I told him and the other glider pilots, "This is where I get off!" I offered the driver my hand grenades, because I had no more use for them. He thanked me and wished me luck. I got out of the truck and told the other pilots that each of us had his orders to return to England—and each of us must choose our own way. They chose to stay with the truck. I walked away.

I made my way toward the trolley car, which had stopped and was very crowded. I unloaded my machine gun, but left it slung over my shoulder. I aimed it at the open door. The crowd moved back and gave me lots of room as I stepped aboard. I had no Belgian money and could not pay for my ride. It never became an issue.

The trolley was passing what looked like a U.S.O. club located in the central part of the city. Army personnel were moving in and out. It looked inviting, and I thought perhaps I could get something eat. So, I got off at the next stop.

I walked back to the U.S.O. and went in. Sure enough, it was a type of mess hall. I ordered some coffee and a muffin, and was looking for a place to sit, when I spotted my CO sitting at a table with Major Stovall. I stared in disbelief; I was sure they had been killed!

I went over, sat down and told them I never thought I would see them again. The CO looked beat. His uniform was practically in rags. Major Stovall seemed to be in fine shape; he said he ejected through the front window of his plane. My CO, a full colonel said, "Bagley, do you have any sugar?" I answered, "I always carry sugar for the Colonel." As I handed him a handful of sugar cubes, I said, "With compliments from the women of Eindhoven."

After finishing my light breakfast, I excused myself and headed for the Brussels airport. I grabbed another streetcar, made a transfer and was there. I walked onto the apron near the terminal building, praying I would see a stranded or parked Dakota. I passed a couple of hangars, walked down a taxi way, rounded a corner and lo and behold, there was a Dakota, with its starboard wheel stuck about two feet down in the mud. The starboard engine prop was almost touching the surface of the concrete taxi strip. I found the crew chief on board and asked him where the pilot was. He said, "Over at administration." I told him it was necessary that I see him right away. We went over to the administration office, located the pilot and I introduced myself. I asked him, "If I get your plane out of the mud, will you take me and a dozen or so glider pilots to England, around the Nottingham area?" He said, "Yeah, sure." So I told him, "Go back to the plane and wait. I'll be back in no more than half an hour."

I located three glider pilots in the waiting area of the administration building. They were easily identifiable because of their battle jackets. I explained to them what I had in mind. I asked each of them to find three more glider pilots and meet me back in the waiting room.

It wasn't long before there were fifteen glider pilots assembled. I informed them that when we got this plane out of the mud, the pilot had promised to fly each of us to his respective field in England.

"OK," I said, "let's go. Follow my instructions." I got the Dakota pilot, crew chief and glider pilots assembled outside the aircraft, and explained what was to be the sequence of events. "I want three of you on the port side of the tail section. You are to push the tail towards the starboard side. The rest of you are to get under the starboard wing and push up as far as possible to lift that wheel out of the mud. The pilot is to start only the starboard engine. I know the blade tip is close to the ground, but the mud is hard, so the plane will not sink any farther. Put the prop in low pitch for maximum thrust. Unlock the tail wheel, so it can rotate. Put the flaps all the way down for maximum lift." I gestured towards the Dakota pilot. "After the engine is warmed up, his signal to begin using lifting and pushing will be the deployment of full flaps. You men lifting on the wing; lift to the rear— and keep away from the prop!"

The pilot and glider pilots followed the instructions perfectly. The flaps came down and we lifted the wing to almost level. Slowly, the tail section started to move, and soon the wheel was back on the cement.

The Dakota pilot started the port engine and we all piled in. The plane did not carry parachutes except for the pilot, co-pilot and crew chief. So once again, we glider pilots had no chutes. Well, I thought, if it really came down to it, we could shut down the engines and fly it like a glider.

Soon we passed the White Cliffs of Dover from seaward, and I felt we were home again. I was the last glider pilot delivered on that flight. I thanked the Dakota crew and watched as they took off and climbed into the sunset.

Then I went over to see Chaplain McArthur; we played a game of chess.

Chapter 11

FLYING THE XCG-13A

Achiet, France

During the winter of 1944, our division moved into France, to a new location called B54[16]. It was a former Spitfire base. I was given the task of flying General Gavin's car and driver in Grantham. We landed safely and unloaded the car. The driver asked me what I was going to do next.

"Not much," I replied.

He asked me if I would like to be driven to Paris in the General's car.

"That would be great," I said.

So there I was, riding around Paris in a two-star general's car! We were getting salutes from all the military men along the street.

Finally, I decided the fun was over and told the driver to take me back to B54. I needed to find out where I was supposed to be billeted. Oh how the MPs at the main gate came to attention when we drove in! They didn't even ask who we were.

At B54 there was a beautiful chateau where we set up our engineering offices. What a letdown to find out where I was billeted. It was an old wood building, with each room big enough to hold twelve officers and all their equipment. I was assigned a bunk next to a guy named Groveman, who I had known for several years.

Next, I found out where the mess hall and the officers' club were. I then went down to the Engineering Office in the chateau and posted status reports on some 100 gliders.

---

[16] At Achiet, the Advanced Landing Ground (ALG) B54 was one of the temporary airfields constructed by Allied forces in Normandy in the days following the D-Day landings. ALGs enabled the relocation of tactical air support from England to Normandy, shortening the turnaround time from the front lines. (Source: Wikipedia)

I found an order on my desk to pick up five gliders in England and bring them back to B54. I took my crew chief along to help inspect the new gliders, which we picked up at the sub-depot. We inspected all of them, and none of them was in acceptable condition. They had been grounded due to various technical orders.

I went to the colonel in charge of the sub-depot. He asked if I was ready to pick up the gliders.

"Not really," I said. "Have you got any others to choose from?"

"That's all I have right now."

A lieutenant called out to me from the back of the room. "If you don't want those gliders, I'll take them!"

"You're welcome to them," I replied.

I told my crew chief that we would be returning to France without a damn thing. Five DC-3s had made the trip to England, each expecting to return with a glider in tow. I knew I would have some explaining to do to the base commander.

The next day I posted my status report, indicating what my crew chief and I had found wrong with each of the gliders. But Command still called and wanted to know why we had refused to pick them up. I explained to Captain Myers that each of them had grounding technical orders, and therefore did not meet Air Force flight regulations. In addition, that they should have all been grounded by the sub-depot. I told him I had a list each glider's serial number and outstanding technical order.

Captain Myers sent that list up through the channels to Command. Eventually, I was ordered to fly back to England and pick up five gliders not grounded by technical orders. This time, the sub-depot gave us five brand new gliders, manufactured by Ford. They were the best CG-4A gliders ever built!

I took those five gliders back to the base, and assigned one to the 29th Squadron, one to the 37th, one to the 38th, and two to the 49th. We entered a status report that said all gliders were flyable.

To my consternation, Command decided to transfer all the new CG-4As to another group shortly thereafter. In their place, we were given a much bigger glider, the Waco XCG-13A, which held forty passengers and was equipped with an automatic pilot, tricycle landing gear and gyro.

These larger birds came to us with an instruction manual and an autopilot in a kit requiring assembly. We had to make sure that the rope angle detector was installed correctly, so the glider could accurately track the tow plane. This was accomplished by a three-element control system that involved the ailerons, rudder and elevator controls. To generate enough electricity to run the autopilot, we had batteries on board and electric generators manually operated on the exterior.

Around the same time that we got the larger glider, the DC-3 tow planes were replaced with the larger Curtis Commandos, or C-46s. They had two decks and were at that time the most powerful twin-engine plane in the world.

Since I had never flown such a huge glider, I couldn't wait to take it for a test run. I wanted to simulate how it would handle the forty passengers, so I decided to add sandbags equal in weight to forty fully outfitted paratroopers.

Tom Crouse was in the C-46, ready to tow me down the runway. "OK," I said. "Let's roll!"

Just as we began to move, about ten guys decided they wanted to take a joyride and jumped in. Tom opened the throttle and we rolled down the runway. Even though he now had the more powerful airplane, I could see that Tom was not building up enough speed to get off the ground in time. The end of the runway was coming up fast. I was barely airborne, flying about five feet above the tow plane. I told Tom to feel free to cut me loose at any time.

"Bagley, what the hell do you have in that glider?"

I told him about the 10,000 pounds of sandbags and the ten guys who had jumped on board at the last minute.

"Well," he said, "were you going to say anything? That could make a difference."

We continued down the runway, but Tom did not cut us loose. He said, "I can make it. I'm off the ground and putting my landing gear up, but we have to be careful which direction we turn. If we go left, the tow rope is going to hit the church steeple."

"OK by me," I replied. In turning right, we managed to avoid taking out the steeple and some other tall buildings as well.

When we got to 5,000 feet I told Tom I wanted to go back to the field. With the extra weight, the glider was a bit on the heavy side. He towed us back and we cut loose at 3,000 feet.

I was wondering how this heavy aircraft would land. I just let it glide in, with very little intervention on my part. Fortunately, it turned out to be a smooth and easy landing. All ten guys were elated to be back on the ground safely, especially after I informed them that we had exceeded the weight capacity of the glider.

The next several days I spent perfecting the autopilot. I followed the instructions to a "t" and made all the necessary connections.

Just as I finished the set-up, I got word from Wing Command: "Do not use the autopilot on the XCG-13As." At that stage, this was irritating to hear, so I decided to test it anyway. I called Tom and asked if he could take me up. He said he would be ready for hookup in a few minutes.

Tom taxied over and towed me with the C-46. I began flying manually, with no autopilot at that point. Tom suggested we go up to 3,000 feet; I would then turn it on and see what happened next.

At 3,000 feet, I engaged the rudder control. Because the wings stayed straight, I set the dial to zero. The next adjustment I made was the elevator control, which determines the altitude of the glider with respect to the tow plane. Initially, the glider dropped below the tow plane by about fifty feet, so I adjusted the dial and brought the glider to fifty feet above it, which was where I wanted to be. Next, I set the aileron control. The aileron keeps the wings level.

I told Tom, "The autopilot is on, so let's try making a turn."

Tom made a left hand banking turn, and the glider did the same, tracking the tow plane perfectly.

"OK Tom, that was pretty good. Now I'm going to cut off and try it on my own, with the autopilot engaged."

I cut loose and nothing unusual happened; the glider flew straight and level. I turned the dial 10°, and made a precise 10° turn to the left. Then I straightened it out and adjusted the dial to go into a 10° right hand turn. Once again, the glider made a perfect turn. I performed some other maneuvers; the glider performed impeccably.

With the autopilot still on, I brought the glider in for a landing. When I was twenty feet from the ground, I went manual and we touched down for a perfect landing. That was the second time I had flown that glider, and I enjoyed every minute of it. To this day, I cannot understand the order not to engage the autopilot.

I thought the reason these larger gliders and C-46s were assigned to our group was because they were going to be used for transporting troops and supplies to the Berlin Airlift. But to my knowledge, the forty-passenger gliders were never used on any mission. On the other hand, the C-46 was used in every theatre of the war, most famous for its operations in the Far East including "Flying the Hump"—transporting supplies to troops in China from bases in India and Burma.

After several weeks of no activity at our base, I noticed the 100 C-46s assigned to our group were loaded with paratroopers getting ready to take off on some secret mission. The planes were taking off on runway 17. This runway was known to have strong crosswinds blowing from right to left. An experienced pilot would start his takeoff on the extreme right-hand side, and allow for weathervaning; just as the name suggests, they could end up on the opposite side of the runway before they could get airborne.

Around twenty C-46s got off safely. Then, one pilot started his takeoff too close to the left-hand side. His plane began to weathervane badly and he completely lost control of the aircraft. We watched in horror, anticipating what was about to happen. There was total chaos on the field, as everyone began running helter-skelter for cover. The C-46 crashed into several ambulances, fire trucks and emergency vehicles parked along the edge of the runway. The pilot found himself about twenty feet in the air atop a pile of crushed vehicles. Miraculously, no one was injured. This disaster did not stop the remaining C-46s from taking off safely—from the extreme right-hand side of the runway, however.

Once airborne, they stayed in formation over the airfield, awaiting their orders. Once received, all the C-46s began to move out, heading for Bastogne and the Battle of the Bulge.

After dropping paratroopers into Bastogne, the returning planes from the 313th were shot up badly, and we lost twenty percent of our C-46s on that mission. Unfortunately, the C-46s were very susceptible to small arms fire. With over 7,000 feet of hydraulic tubing, combustion would prove to be a serious problem.

One incident I remember vividly involved leaking hydraulic fluid. The plane had been hit by small arms fire and was leaking badly. The pilot refused to land, because he was afraid the plane would blow up when it hit the runway. The CO, realizing that this plane had better get on the ground pretty quick, ordered the pilot to land the damn thing in the grass.

"No, I can't do that, Sir," said the pilot. "There are unexploded German bombs in the grass."

The Colonel then told the pilot to make a belly landing on the runway.

"No, Sir, I refuse," he replied. "It's too risky to make any attempt to land this crate. I'm going to take her up to 10,000 feet and we are going to bail out!"

The crew jumped first, then the pilot. Their parachutes opened perfectly. The pilot had put the plane on autopilot, heading it in the direction of the English Channel, hoping it would crash into the water. However, the plane had other plans. It began circling the field, diving, barely missing several structures. After about fifteen minutes, it began making low, sweeping turns closer and closer to the ground. It finally crashed into a barn, killing an unlucky cow in the process.

❖   ❖   ❖

One day I received an urgent call from Command. I was told that General Eisenhower needed aviation-grade fuel for Patton's tanks, as his supply was running low. Patton had been ordered to turn his army at Nancy and head toward Bastogne.

Major Jake Myers, the Group Engineering Officer, asked me, "Mark, do you know where we can find any aviation fuel? General Patton needs gasoline for his tanks."

"Yes," I said. "We have about 2,000 gallons out here in drums. British Petroleum has been delivering ten barrels every day since the Brits pulled out of their former Spitfire base. All this time I've had my sergeant roll the barrels into the field and put them where no one can see them. I wanted the extra fuel for the possibility of testing engines at the sub-depot."

That was all Major Myers needed to hear. The next thing I knew there were several hundred DC-3s landing at B54. They were anxious to pick up the fuel that I had been squirreling away to get it to Patton, to use in his tanks at Bastogne.

Chapter 12

GOING HOME

Hollywood, California

About a week after Operation Overlord[17] ended, troops started for home. The Air Force asked if I would be willing to fly a war-weary airplane home to the U.S. I told them it was a little late.

"No," I said, "I choose to go home by steamer."

One week later, I was aboard the S.S. *General Richardson* in the middle of the Atlantic Ocean bound for New York. Violent storms generated off the coast of Florida had traveled north, hitting us head on in the open ocean. The ship's captain did his best to keep us on course. At one point, a "super wave" rose up out of the ocean and swamped the ship. Everyone on deck held on for dear life to anything they could grab—except for the forty men who washed overboard never to be seen or heard from again. Eventually, the rest of us arrived safe and somewhat sound in New York City.

The next leg of my journey home was from New York to Boston. Fortunately, this leg was uneventful. In Boston, I boarded a train at the South Station bound for Taunton, Massachusetts.

The train went right by my house, and I caught a glimpse of my dad working out back and our old Hudson parked in the driveway. If the train had been going a little slower, I could have jumped off and saved myself some time. However, this was not the case, and after about an hour, the train arrived at Taunton A.F.B. There, I applied for and received a twenty-four-hour leave. I grabbed my duffel bag and started to thumb a ride. Good fortune was on my side as a truck

---

[17] "Operation Overlord" was the code name for the Allied invasion of N.W. Europe, which began on D-Day and ended when Allied forces pushed across the River Seine.

picked me up within no time at all, and delivered me to my home in East Foxboro.

My dad was out hoeing the garden about ten feet from our back door, and thirty feet from where the truck left me off. He saw me as the truck pulled away and I thought he would run over and give me a hug—but no. He left the hoe standing and ran for the back door screaming for my mother, "Mary, Mary, Mark is home!"

My mom and dad rushed out the back door and we ran towards each other. When we all met up, I hugged them and they hugged me. Then my sisters Louise and Marie ran out to greet me with big hugs as well.

For dinner that evening, my mom prepared a special treat for me. She fixed a roast beef dinner with Yorkshire pudding, my favorite. It had been five years since I had enjoyed such a grand dinner!

After dinner, my little sister, Louise, lit up a cigarette. That upset my dad, so I figured if I had one, too, it would just make him angrier. So, no after-dinner smoke for me.

We all had a wonderful evening talking, and went to bed late. The next morning I visited the Foxboro Company and saw my former coworkers. After that, Marie drove me to Taunton, just in time to catch the train to California. We were billeted in a standard railroad car for the seven days to Camp Beale.[18] We all expected that at some point the train would stop and we would be transferred to an express Pullman class train, but it never happened.

Our train moved at a snail's pace—about 35 mph over bumpy tracks used by freight trains. Two baggage cars converted into kitchens served the 800 pilots on board. The food was terrible. I think the German prisoners of war got better treatment than we did as returning U.S. AAF pilots! They were given the best accommodations—air conditioned Pullman trains. We on the other hand, could have used some air conditioning while traveling through the desert Southwest. But we tried to make the best of the situation.

When we arrived at Camp Beale, we were told we could leave the base that night if we applied for a leave of absence. But if we waited

---

[18] About forty miles north of Sacramento, CA, Camp Beale opened in October 1942 as a training site for the 13th Armored and the 81st and 96th Infantry Divisions. During WWII, Camp Beale's 86,000 acres were home to more than 60,000 soldiers, a POW encampment and a 1,000-bed hospital. In 1948, the camp transferred from the Army to the Air Force. (Source: www.militarymuseum.org)

until the following day, we would get our discharge from the military. I chose the latter.

The next day, I reported to a major for my discharge papers. He asked me if I wanted to join the National Guard. I told him if I could fly every day for the rest of my life I would join, but if he could not guarantee that . . . then my answer was not only "No," but "Hell, no, Sir!"

The Major wrote in my final paperwork, "Not recommended for National Guard duty." He then gave me my Honorable Discharge.

I immediately boarded the bus for Los Angeles. When I arrived, I called my wife. She had rented a nice apartment on Beachwood Drive in Hollywood. Mary answered the phone, then realizing it was me gasped, "Where are you?"

"Hollywood and Vine," I said.

"I'll meet you there in ten minutes!" she said. "I have a black Ford."

We went to my mother and father-in-law's apartment for a wonderful dinner of ham, baked beans with brown bread and homemade apple pie for dessert—another of my favorites!

After dinner, Mary and I drove to the apartment she had rented for us and we did not come out for three days. Nine months later the apple of my eye, my daughter Susan, was born.

The author (2nd from left) with his family, on the beach near Cape Cod, circa 1965. Left to right: Mary (wife), Mark, Agnes (sister), Mary (mother), Susan (daughter) and John (brother)

EPILOGUE

After he was discharged from the service, my uncle, Mark Bagley, bought a basic trainer and flew solo from Los Angeles to Massachusetts, where he soon returned to work at the Foxboro Company. There, he became the director of the Field Trial Deparment. But opportunities out West were calling, so he, Mary and their daughter, Susan, returned to California, where he went to work for the Bechtel Corporation. Over the next fourteen years with Bechtel, he showed a wide range of expertise in the petrochemical, power, aerospace, nuclear and international divisions. While in the international division, he spent a year in Saudi Arabia, working on the design and control systems for the Trans-Arabian oil pipeline. He was also one of forty selected to spend three years in France, using his expertise in control systems design to install an oil pipeline there. He later spent three years in Belgium, as a consultant to the Corning Glass Company.

Mark then traveled to Houston, Texas, where he designed the control systems for automation and computer safety for the man-rated space simulation chamber at NASA. Although NASA offered him a position, he preferred to return to California to work for the Ralph M. Parsons Company in Pasadena. There, he served in the power division as the Chief Control Systems Engineer and was responsible for the control systems design and philosophy at the Hyperion power plant in Los Angeles. On evenings and weekends, he taught classes in controls and measurement at Los Angeles Harbor College.

Mark's contributions greatly developed the Control Systems discipline in engineering; he is attributed with establishing the Registered Professional Control Systems Engineer designation. In 1984, the Southern California Meter Association named him Engineer of the Year. He later served as president of both the SCMA and the Instrument Society of America.

Because of his accomplishments as a Registered Professional Control Engineer, Nuclear Engineer and Manufacturing Engineer, he served many times as an Expert Examiner for the State of California in Control Systems Engineering.

After retiring at the age of 72, he bought a powerboat, the *Dulcinea*, and kept her moored at the Long Beach Harbor marina. He kept up his commercial pilot's license, until macular degeneration made it impossible to fly any longer.

In 1994, he and Mary moved to Las Vegas to live closer to Susan and her husband. Mark Bagley passed away on December 30, 2006 at age 88.

-Marianne Stephens

Mark Bagley (left) at the Foxboro Company in 1952

APPENDIX

T he following pages contain images of a number of official U.S. Army letters and papers belonging to Mark B. Bagley.

World War II memorial as it stands today in East Foxboro, Massachusetts. Author's name is on far left, seventh from top

CHARACTER OF SEPARATION Honorable	TRANSCRIPT OF MILITARY RECORD		DEPARTMENT Army
1. LAST NAME – FIRST NAME – MIDDLE INITIAL Bagley Mark B		2. SERVICE NUMBER T 60 366	3. GRADE AND DATE OF RANK F/O 15 Dec 42
4. ORGANIZATION Carrier Gp 49th Troop Carrier Sq 313th Troop		5. COMPONENT AUS	6. ARM OR SERVICE AC
7. DATE OF DISCHARGE OR SEPARATION 4 Nov 44	8. PLACE OF SEPARATION APO 133		
9. DATE OF BIRTH 26 Feb 18	10. PLACE OF BIRTH Boston Mass		

11. DATE OF INDUCTION — 12. DATE OF ENLISTMENT — 13. DATE OF ENTRY INTO ACTIVE SVC 15 Dec 42 — 14. PLACE OF ENTRY INTO SERVICE Stout Field Ind

15. RACE White — 16. MARITAL STATUS MARRIED x — 17. U.S. CITIZEN YES x — 18. CIVILIAN OCCUPATION AND NO. Teacher 33.410

SELECTIVE SERVICE DATA — 19. REGISTERED NO x — 20. LOCAL S.S. BOARD NO. — 21. COUNTY AND STATE 119 Norfolk Mass — 22. HOME ADDRESS East St East Foxboro Mass

23. MILITARY OCCUPATIONAL SPECIALTY AND NO. Glider Pilot 1026 — 24. MILITARY QUALIFICATION AND DATE Aviation Badge Glider Pilot

25. BATTLES AND CAMPAIGNS
Naples-Foggia Normandy Northern France Rhineland Rome-Arno Sicily

26. DECORATIONS, MEDALS, BADGES, COMMENDATIONS, CITATIONS, AND CAMPAIGN RIBBONS AWARDED OR AUTHORIZED
Air Medal European-African-Middle Eastern Campaign Medal w/1 Silver Star & 1 Bronze Service Star American Campaign Medal Distinguished Unit Citation Emblem w/1 Oak Leaf Cluster

27. WOUNDS RECEIVED IN ACTION
None

28. TOTAL LENGTH OF ACTIVE SERVICE THIS PERIOD: CONTINENTAL SERVICE 0 years 4 months 28 days; FOREIGN SERVICE 1 year 5 months 22 days
30. SERVICE OUTSIDE CONTINENTAL U.S. AND RETURN: DATE OF DEPARTURE 13 May 43 DESTINATION EAMETO DATE OF ARRIVAL 20 May 43

31. PRIOR SERVICE

32. REASON AND AUTHORITY FOR SEPARATION
To accept a commission

33. SERVICE SCHOOLS ATTENDED
None

34. REMARKS
Blood Group A

Given by the Department of the Army, Washington, D. C., on 6 March 1953

To be completed for enlisted personnel only.

TAGO FORM 01254
1 NOV 52   REPLACES AGO FORM 01254, 1 AUG 51, WHICH IS OBSOLETE.   GPO 83-43708

Appendix

HEADQUARTERS
82ND SERVICE GROUP
Group Engineering Office

APO 149, U.S. Army.
1 September 1944.

SUBJECT: Recommendation for Appointment to 2nd Lt., AUS.

TO   : Whom it may concern.

    1. It is with pleasure that the undersigned officer recommends F/O Mark B. Bagley, T-60366, Group Glider Officer, 49th Troop Carrier Squadron, 313th Troop Carrier Group, APO 133, on application to 2nd Lieutenant, Army United States.

    2. Pursuant to a daily association in the past five months, in the performance of Glider Engineering activities, subject Flight Officer has proven to be exemplary in the efficient and conscientious performance of duty so duly assigned. He has demonstrated outstanding ability in the capacity to accomplish the task at hand augmented with the courteousness and military bearing that demands the respect and is in true keeping with tradition of the service.

    3. It is the firm belief of the undersigned, that subject Flight Officer would be of more value to the service as a commissioned officer than in the present status.

HARRY BROWN,
Major, Air Corps,
Gp. Engineering Officer.

173

HEADQUARTERS SEVENTH ARMY
A. P. O. #758, U. S. ARMY

27 October 1943.

SUBJECT: Commendation.

TO   : Brigadier General Paul L. Williams, Troop Carrier Command.

        The demonstration at Ponte Olivio and Comiso Airfields, as executed by your command on 25 October 1943, of loading, dropping by parachute, and landing, was the best that it has been my privilege to witness. The towing and landing of the gliders, the dropping by parachute of the personnel of the 82d Airborne Division, the assembling and putting into action of heavy equipment, was executed with a dispatch and proficiency evidencing a high state of planning, discipline and training.

        I wish to commend you and all personnel connected with this demonstration for their outstanding performance.

G. S. PATTON, JR.,
Lieutenant General, U. S. Army,
Commanding.

HEADQUARTERS
313TH TROOP CARRIER GROUP ACP
OFFICE OF THE ENGINEERING OFFICER

APO 133, U.S. Army.
31 August, 1944.

SUBJECT: Recommendation of F/O MARK B. BAGLEY.

TO   : Whom it may concern.

F/O MARK B. BAGLEY, (T-60366), has worked under my direct
supervision in the capacity of Group Glider Engineering Officer for the
past year.

He has shown initiative and sound judgement in his work, and
his performance of duty has been superior. I believe that F/O BAGLEY
is fully qualified to become a commissioned officer and recommend that
favorable consideration be given his application for a commission as
Second Lieutenant in the Army of the United States.

JACOB J. MYERS, JR.
Major, Air Corps,
Gp. Engineering O.

HEADQUARTERS
IX TROOP CARRIER COMMAND

G-H-1

APO 133, U.S. Army,
6 November 1944

GENERAL ORDERS)
:
NUMBER 107)

E X T R A C T

SECTION I: AWARDS OF THE AIR MEDAL

* * * *

SECTION I

* * * *

2. By direction of the President, Under the provisions of Executive Order Number 9158 (Bull 25, WD 1942), as amended by Executive Order Number 9242-A (Bull 49, WD 1942) and in accordance with authority delegated by the War Department, and pursuant to authority contained in letter, file 200.6, Headquqrters, United States Strategic Air Forces in Europe, Subject: "Awards and Decorations", dated 8 September 1944, an AIR MEDAL is awarded to the following named Officers, organizations and residence as indicated, for meritorious achievement while partiàipating in aerial flights during the period 17 September 1944 to 23 September 1944. As Troop Carrier Glider pilots, these Officers demonstrated exceptional airmanship and resolution in the execution of missions vital to the vertical envelopment of enemy positions in Holland. Piloting their gliders over extended routes in difficult weather, and braving hails of flak and small-arms fire, they successfully landed thousands of airborne troops and huge quantities of combat equipment and supplies at designated objectives behind enemy lines. Their outstanding achievements in the greatest airborne operation in military history reflect the highest credit upon the military forces of the United States:

* * * *

313TH TROOP CARRIER GROUP

* * * *

49TH Troop Carrier Squadron

* * * *

MARK B. BAGLEY T 60 366 F/O Foxboro, Mass.

* * * *

By command of Major General WILLIAMS:

JAMES E. DUKE, JR
Colonel, GSC
Chief of Staff

OFFICIAL:

S/ O.W. Howland
t/ O.W. HOWLAND
Colonel, A G D
Adjutant General

THIS IS A TRUE EXTRACT COPY:

Jacob J. Myers, Jr.
JACOB J. MYERS, JR.,
Major, Air Corps.

R E S T R I C T E D

Appendix

The Air Medal awarded to Mark Bagley on 8 September 1944, "...for meritorious achievement while participating in aerial flights during the period 17 September 1944 to 23 September 1944...demonstrated exceptional airmanship and resolution in the execution of missions vital to the vertical envelopment of enemy positions in Holland." (See page 176) *Photo by Nicole M. Parker*

THIS FORM WILL NOT BE REPLACED
IF LOST OR DESTROYED. SAVE IT

ARMY

SEPARATION QUALIFICATION RECORD

LAST NAME - FIRST NAME - MIDDLE INITIAL	ARMY SERIAL NUMBER	GRADE	DATE OF ENTRY INTO ACTIVE SERVICE	SEX	DATE OF BIRTH
BAGLEY MARK B	01 996 295	2dLt	5 Nov 42	M	26 Feb 18

PERMANENT ADDRESS FOR MAILING PURPOSES (Street and Number - City - County - State)
1829 N. Beachwood Street Hollywood Los Angeles County California

CIVILIAN EDUCATION

HIGHEST GRADE COMPLETED	LAST YEAR OF ATTENDANCE	HIGHEST DEGREE RECEIVED	MAJOR COURSE OF STUDY	NAME AND ADDRESS OF LAST SCHOOL ATTENDED
12	1938	None	Engineering	Mass. Institute of Tech. Boston, Mass.

OTHER TRAINING OR SCHOOLING

COURSE	NO.MOS.	COURSE	NO.MOS.	COURSE	NO.MOS.	COURSE	NO.MOS.
None							

SERVICE EDUCATION

SERVICE SCHOOL	COURSE	MOS	RATING	ARMY SPECIALIZED TRAINING PROGRAM		
				INSTITUTION WHERE ENROLLED	CURRICULUM AND TERM (COURSE OF TRAINING PURSUED)	NO. OF WEEKS	GRADUATED YES NO
AAFAFS	Advanced Flying	13	Grad	None		

CIVILIAN OCCUPATIONS

MAIN OCCUPATION (TITLE) **TEACHER**   SECONDARY OCCUPATION (TITLE) **AIRPLANE PILOT COMMERCIAL**

JOB SUMMARY
Instructor in temperature and humidity, pressure, etc.

JOB SUMMARY
Flew passengers for hire.

NO.OF YEARS	LAST DATE OF EMPLOYMENT	NAME AND ADDRESS OF EMPLOYER	NO.OF YEARS	LAST DATE OF EMPLOYMENT	NAME AND ADDRESS OF EMPLOYER
5	1942	Foxboro Instrument Co Foxboro, Mass.	1	1941	Self-employed

MILITARY SPECIALTIES

ASSIGNMENTS

YEARS	MONTHS	GRADE	PRINCIPAL DUTY	ARMY CODE NO	YEARS	MONTHS	GRADE	PRINCIPAL DUTY	ARMY CODE NO
2	6	2dLt	Glider Pilot	1026					

SUMMARY OF MILITARY OCCUPATION (Shown by title)

Instructed student glider pilots for 3 months; tested planes for Boeing Aircraft (Army acceptance Test Pilot); was group glider engineering officer during overseas service.

SUMMARY OF MILITARY OCCUPATION AND CIVILIAN CONVERSIONS (Shown by title)

° THIS INFORMATION BASED ON SOLDIER'S STATEMENT. (Indicate by * any items not supported by military records)

DATE OF SEPARATION	SIGNATURE OF SOLDIER	SIGNATURE OF SEPARATION CLASSIFICATION OFFICER
24 Sept 45	Mark B Bagley	J. B. ROONEY CAPTAIN AC

W.D.,A.G.O. FORM NO. 100   15 July 1944

ASF-NSC Separation Center
Camp Beale, Calif.

THE

PRESIDENT

OF

THE UNITED STATES OF AMERICA

To all who shall see these presents, greeting:

Know Ye, that reposing special trust and confidence in the patriotism, valor, fidelity and abilities of Mark Bernard Bagley

I do appoint him, temporarily, Second Lieutenant

in

The Army of the United States

such appointment to date from the fifth *day of* November *nineteen hundred and* forty-four *He is therefore carefully and diligently to discharge the duty of the office to which he is appointed by doing and performing all manner of things thereunto belonging.*

And I do strictly charge and require all Officers and Soldiers under his command when he shall be employed on active duty, to be obedient to his orders as an officer of his grade and position. And he is to observe and follow such orders and directions, from time to time, as he shall receive from me, or the future President of the United States of America, or the General or other Superior Officers set over him, according to the rules and discipline of War.

This commission to continue in force during the pleasure of the President of the United States for the time being and for the duration of the present emergency and for six months thereafter unless sooner terminated.

Done at the City of Washington, this thirteenth *day of* March *in the year of our Lord one thousand nine hundred and* forty-seven *, and of the Independence of the United States of America the one hundred and* seventy-first

By the President:

Major General,
The Adjutant General.

179

Printed in the United States
130443LV00001B/225/P

9 781555 716578